THE PROMISED REDEEMER

THE FULFILLMENT AND HISTORICAL AUTHENTICITY OF MESSIANIC PROPHECY

Roger Liebi

Christlicher Medienvertrieb Hagedorn
Postfach 30 04 30
40404 Düsseldorf
Germany

Scipture quotations were taken from the King James Version/
Authorised Version.

Copyright © 2014 by CMV Hagedorn
Original title: *Der verheißene Erlöser*
2015 Second Edition
CMV · Christlicher Medienvertrieb Hagedorn
Postfach 30 04 30
40404 Düsseldorf
Germany
info@cmv-video.de
www.cmv-duesseldorf.de

Translation: Timothy Capes
Cover and layout: Susanne Martin

Print: www.arkadruk.pl
ISBN: 978-3-943175-32-5

Contents

Introduction

In order to be able to deal with Messianic prophecy in detail, it is necessary to establish some of the basic facts regarding the origin and transmission of the Old Testament (OT).

The OT was written in Hebrew and in Aramaic over a period in excess of 1000 years. The oldest parts of the OT were written at the latest during the time of Moses (around 1600 BC).[1] The book of the prophet Malachi is the last document in the OT, originating in around 420 BC.

When reading through the OT in its entirety, one gains a profound sense of the yearning and longing for the coming Saviour, the Messiah, who would provide a solution for mankind's problems, and bring in everlasting righteousness. This promised Messiah is described in minute detail on the OT. Amazingly there are many passages in the OT referring to a "*suffering Messiah*" who would be hated and rejected by His own people, and who would be killed by the most dreadful means, and in doing so would suffer for the sins of many. On the other hand a "*victorious Messiah*" is spoken of, who, at his arrival, would bring about a worldwide, glorious reign of peace. How should the tension between these different descriptions of the one Messiah be resolved without contradiction? This apparent paradox is easily resolved when it is observed that both of these different descriptions deal with two appearances, separated in time, of one and the same Messiah.

The prophecies dealing with the "triumphant Messiah" are yet future for us, whereas those describing the "suffering Messiah" have been completely fulfilled in the past.

This is a question of dealing with over 330 precise, but definitively individual, prophecies. In the following, it will be proved with historical evidence that they were literally fulfilled in the historical Jesus of Nazareth. Before doing so, however, we must demonstrate that it is impossible that these prophecies are in any way counterfeits introduced later.

Between 1947 and 1956, Biblical manuscripts were discovered in eleven caves of Qumran at the Dead Sea,[2] causing an unprecedented sensation throughout the world. In these scrolls, which in part originate from pre-Christian times, all the books of the OT are documented except the book of Esther.

Since the majority of the Messianic prophecies is to be found in the book of the prophet Isaiah the discovery of a complete Isaiah scroll is of great significance. The text is written on goatskin parchment in unvocalized Hebrew. The scroll, made of parchment sewn together from 17 goat skins, is 7.34m (24') long, and 26cm (10¼") wide. This scroll's amazingly good condition of preservation is quite sensational.

This manuscript was dated to around 125 BC on the basis of palaeographic tests as well as Carbon-14 dating techniques at the Technical College in Zurich.[3] Many years ago Prof. Dr. André Lamorte quite rightly gave his judgment on the age of this scroll: "The complete Isaiah scroll is regarded today as having been copied down before the Christian era began. The experts in this field diverge in their views generally between the start of the first century to the end of the second century BC".[4]

Since all the Messianic passages in the Book of Isaiah are contained in this scroll, it is absolutely impossible to doubt their authenticity.

This scroll is now the official property of the State of Israel. It was photographed full-scale and put on public display in its entirety. For those who are interested it is now available in this format in the book "Scrolls from Qumran Cave I."[5]

Likewise the authenticity of the Messianic prophecies from the other books in the OT can be documented by the manuscripts of the Dead Sea Scrolls. Frank Moore Cross writes in his book "The Ancient Library of Qumran, and Modern Biblical Studies," that the discovery of these manuscripts renders impossible the placing of any book from the 'former' or the 'latter' prophets (let alone the Pentateuch) to later than the early second century BC.[6]

To the books of the 'former' prophets belong the books of Joshua, Judges, 1 & 2 Samuel, and 1 & 2 Kings, while to the 'latter' prophets belong the books of Isaiah, Jeremiah, Ezekiel, Hosea, Joel, Amos, Obadiah, Jonah, Micah, Nahum, Habakkuk, Zephaniah, Haggai, Zachariah, and Malachi. The Pentateuch contains all of the five books of Moses (Genesis, Exodus, Leviticus, Numbers and Deuteronomy). Thus it is clear that all these books were written in the pre-Christian era.

Since in the following many Messianic prophecies from the Psalms will be quoted, I would also like to draw your attention especially to the discovery of a Psalter manuscript dating from the second century BC.[7]

Also, 8 fragments from the book of the prophet Daniel have come to light. These manuscripts originated from caves I, IV, & VI during the period from around 125-50 BC.[8]

As well as these manuscript discoveries from Qumran there is a further proof for the authenticity of the Messianic prophecies: the existence of the Alexandrian Translation of the OT. Start of translation of the entire OT into Greek began around 285 BC, i.e. during the reign of the Egyptian King, Ptolemy II Philadelphus. According to tradition 72 Jewish scholars are said to have worked on this translation, hence it bears the name *Septuagint*.[9]

At the beginning of the second century BC, Aristobulus, a Jew, wrote that the translation of the Law into Greek had been completed in the reign of Ptolemy Philadelphus.[10] The expression "Law" is understood in many cases to be a term for the five books of Moses, or indeed it could also denote the entire OT.[11] From the testimony of Aristobulus it is possible that the entire translation of the entire OT was completed by the end of the third century BC. Anyway it is certain that this was the case by 130 BC at the latest, because it emerges from the prologue from the book of Jesus Sirach, which dates from this period, that the Septuagint translation covered the whole of the OT. It says:

"For the same things uttered in Hebrew, and translated into another tongue, have not the same force in them: and not only these things, but the law itself, and the prophets, and the rest of the books, when they are spoken in their own language."[12] The expression "the law, the prophets, and the rest of the books" is used when someone wants to emphasize that the *entire* OT is meant. The Alexandrian translation is still present today.[13] So if the entire OT was translated from Hebrew into Greek, at the latest in the second century BC, how can the Messianic prophecies be counterfeits from a later period in time?

In order to be able to document the fulfilment of the Messianic prophecies, there are various historical sources at hand. Great importance has to be attached to the Jewish historical writer, Flavius Josephus (37-100 AD), who wrote a great deal on Jewish history from 175 BC to 70 AD in his two works "De bello Judaico" (History of the Jewish Wars)[14] and "Antiquitates Judaicae" (The Antiquities of the Jews).[15] Likewise the sources and testimonies of Tacitus (ca. 55-118 AD), Thallus (52 AD), Tertullian (2nd Century AD), Cassius Dio (2nd/3rd centuries AD), Julius Africanus (3rd century AD), and the Babylonian Talmud,[16] should be given their proper consideration.

However, the greatest importance should undoubtedly be attached to the reports from the New Testament (NT). According to Kurt Aland, the former head of the West German Institute for New Testament Textual Research in Münster, the NT was copied down in c. 5,300 manuscripts.[17] In addition to these there are 9,000 manuscripts of ancient translations, and tens of thousands of Biblical quotes from the so-called church fathers.[18] These texts vouch for the NT having been copied reliably and to the letter. The time-difference between the original autograph and the oldest copied manuscripts amounts to somewhere between 20 and 250 years.[19] Generally this difference for the ancient Greek and Roman Classics amounts to 900-1300 years, and no-one would think of doubting their reliability because of this, although they are founded improbably on a much more slender textual base.

Three of the four Gospels were written before the destruction of Jerusalem (70 AD): Matthew, Mark, and Luke.[20] After they had been written, these Gospels rapidly gained wide acceptance. If there were any statements in these Gospels that did not agree with the historical facts, the Jews would have immediately used this as a weapon against a burgeoning Christianity. Since the historical facts stated in the Gospels were simply not open to dispute, the battle against the first Christians had to take place first and foremost by means of physical persecution. At that point in time it would have been unthinkable that leading men in Judaism of that day, like Nicodemus (a member of the highest court of justice), Saul of Tarsus (a prominent pupil of the Rabbi Gamaliel), Joseph of Arimathea (a member of the leading council of priests in the Temple), or Apollos (a scholar born in Alexandria) would have become Christians, if Christianity had sought to undermine their current faith with erroneous, absurd, dishonest and pseudo-historical facts!

The NT writings, which were all written in the time between 32 and 98 AD, therefore boast an extremely high level of credibility.

When it comes to the Messianic prophecies, it is often argued, that their fulfilment is purely coincidental. On the basis of probabilities it is easy to refute this allegation. Just suppose that the fulfilment of just one of these prophecies had a probability of 1:2 (in reality it is much smaller), then the fulfilment of 50 of these prophecies would be one chance in 1,125,000,000,000,000, i.e. exactly a possibility of 2^{50} cases. Since with Messianic prophecy we are dealing with the fulfilment of over 330 prophecies, the fulfilment of exactly 330 prophecies would result in a probability of 1:2,187 x 10^{99}!

We cannot imagine the size of this number. This calculation makes it clear, however, that with Messianic prophecy it is *impossible* to speak of a coincidental fulfilment.[21]

Finally, some principal points about the Messianic prophecies should be stated:

1. Messianic prophecies are to be found not only in the books of the prophets, but also in the Law of Moses, and the remaining writings of the OT.

2. A distinction must be made between prophecies in which:
   – God is speaking about His Messiah
   – People are talking about the Messiah, and
   – the Messiah Himself speaks.

3. Many OT prophecies are written in the Past Tense, in order to ensure the certainty of them being fulfilled. In this case it is a question of employing the so-called "Prophetic Perfect Tense", being a proper technical term used in the Hebrew grammar.[22]

The "suffering Messiah" and the "Triumphant Messiah" can be found within one and the same passage of the OT.

The Creator of Messianic prophecy is the "Eternal One" ("YHVH" in Hebrew), the God of the Bible. His Hebrew name translates to as near as the "Eternally-existing One" or "the Unchangeable One". It is the designation of the "Existing One," in the absolute sense. He is not subject to the change of the past, present and future, and, thus, in His foreknowledge and prescience He was able to inform the prophets unerringly about what was to come.

The fact of prophecy in no wise excludes the freedom of the human will or decision-making and its attendant responsibility, because the Eternal One has not pre-determined, but only *foreknown* them. Therefore the Bible speaks about "Prognosis" of God (cf. 1 Peter 1:2 and Romans 8:29), i.e. about the foreknowledge or pre-science of God.

The NT demonstrates that it can be "proved" (in the actual sense of the word) through Messianic prophecy that Jesus of Nazareth is indeed the prophesied Messiah. Acts 9:22 and 18:28 report that both Paul and Apollos used this kind of reasoning for the Christian faith against the Jews. In the first case the original Greek word "symbibazo" is used, and in the second the word "deiknymi." "Symbibazo" denotes argumentation based on logical conclusions derived from a wealth of assembled evidence. "Deiknymi" denotes reasoning based on a clear and plain presentation of the arguments.

It cannot be emphasised enough that no other religion apart from Biblical Christianity knows this sort of reasoning.

Chapter 1

The Timing of the Messiah's Coming

1. Daniel's "Seventy Weeks"

Chapter 9 of Daniel is of great significance for Biblical prophecy. It is in this chapter that the exact timing of the coming of the Messiah as Prince is declared.

The Significance of the Expression "Weeks"

The word "shavua" used in the Hebrew text of Daniel 9:25-27 indicates a "*unit of seven*".

In the context of Daniel 9 the word "schavua" – which otherwise indicates a week of seven days – can merely have the meaning of a "unit of 7 years".

Reckoning in weeks of years was hardly anything new for the Israelites in the OT. God had already commanded the people of Israel in the Law of Moses to count in a cycle of weeks of years. Every seven years the land was to be left fallow, and every seven-times-seven years the Jubilee Year had to be celebrated as a "Jubilee" year (cf. Leviticus 25:1-7, 8-13).

Historical Background

During the years 606-582 BC King Nebuchadnezzar deported the Jews to Babylon as prisoners. Jerusalem, the glorious city, was completely destroyed, the Temple of God as well as the palaces were completely razed to the ground and burnt (2 Chronicles 36).

The Exile lasted for 70 years as Jeremiah had predicted (Jeremiah 25:11-12). Daniel was one of those taken captive, and served as a prophet at that time.

The Timing of the Decree Permitting the Rebuilding of Jerusalem

It follows from the first verse of the ninth chapter that the following prophecy concerning the Messiah dates from 539 BC (the first year of the reign of the Median king, Darius, son of Xerxes = 539 BC). Jerusalem was still lying in ruins at this time. In verses 25 and 26 it says:

"Know therefore and understand, that from the going forth of the commandment to restore and to build Jerusalem unto the Messiah the Prince shall be seven weeks, and threescore and two weeks: the street shall be built again, and the wall, even in troublous times. And after threescore and two weeks shall Messiah be cut off, but not for himself: and the people of the prince that shall come shall destroy the city and the sanctuary; and the end thereof shall be with a flood, and unto the end of the war desolations are determined."

In order to emphasize the importance of the exactness of this quote, this prophecy is additionally rendered in a word-for-word translation from the Hebrew:

vetheda	*So know then*
vethaskel	*and understand*
min	*from*

motza	the going out
davar	of the word
lehashiv	to reconstruct
velivnoth	and to rebuild
yerushalayim	Jerusalem
ad	till
mashiach	the Messiah
nagid	the prince
shavu'im	(are) weeks of years
shiv'ah	seven
veshavu'im	and weeks of years
shishim	sixty
ushenayim	and two.
tashuv	There will returned
venivnetha	and be built
rechov	plaza
vecharutz	and trenches
uvetzoq	and indeed in affliction
ha'ittim	of times
veacharai	And after
hashavu'im	the weeks of years
shishim	sixty
ushenayim	and two
yikkareth	will be murdered
mashiach	the Messiah
ve'en	and nothing
lo	(will be left to) him
veha'ir	And the city
vehaqodesh	and the sanctuary
yash'chit	will destroy
am	the people
nagid	of the prince
haba	of the coming-one

From the time at which the decree is given to rebuild the city *until the moment* when the Messiah would come as Prince, 69 (7 + 62) weeks of years (69 x 7 years = 483 years) would pass.

The issuing of this decree, which is of the utmost importance for the history of the people of Israel, is described precisely in Nehemiah 2:1-8:

"And it came to pass in the month Nisan, in the twentieth year of Artaxerxes the king, that wine was before him: and I took up the wine, and gave it unto the king. Now I had not been beforetime sad in his presence. Wherefore the king said unto me, Why is thy countenance sad, seeing thou art not sick? this is nothing else but sorrow of heart. Then I was very sore afraid, and said unto the king, Let the king live for ever: why should not my countenance be sad, when the city, the place of my fathers' sepulchres, lieth waste, and the gates thereof are consumed with fire? Then the king said unto me, For what dost thou make request? So I prayed to the God of heaven. And I said unto the king, If it please the king, and if thy servant have found favour in thy sight, that thou wouldest send me unto Judah, unto the city of my fathers' sepulchres, that I may build it. And the king said unto me, (the queen also sitting by him,) *For how long shall thy journey be? and when wilt thou return? So it pleased the king to send me; and I set him a time. Moreover I said unto the king, If it please the king, let letters be given me to the governors beyond the river, that they may convey me over till I come into Judah; and a letter unto Asaph the keeper of the king's forest, that he may give me timber to make beams for the gates of the palace which appertained to the house, and for the wall of the city, and for the house that I shall enter into. And the king granted me, according to the good hand of my God upon me."*

The date of this decree is indicated by Nehemiah 2:1: "In the month of Nisan, during the twentieth year of the reign of king Artaxerxes" (= Artaxerxes I Longimanus). Artaxerxes ruled from 464 to 423 BC, ascending the throne in February 464. His reign had already begun *de jure* in July 465 (after Xerxes was murdered). So from which date did Nehemiah calculate? As a Persian official he obviously calculated the duration of his lord's reign from July 465. This we can gather from the following facts: According to Nehemiah 1:1 and 2:1, firstly the month of "Kislev" (November/December), and then afterwards the month "Nisan" (March/April) fell in the 20th year of the king's reign. Thus we can see that Nehemiah calculated the 1st year of the reign of his king from *July* 465 BC. Had Nehemiah calculated the reign from *February* 464 BC, this sequence of months would not have been possible. In that case the month Nisan would have come *before* the month Kislev. On the basis of these considerations we can of necessity equate the time given in Nehemiah 2:1 with March/April 445 BC.

Thus for the Israelites in the OT Daniel 9 can be read as follows: that 483 years would elapse from the issuing of the decree for the rebuilding of Jerusalem (March/April 465 BC), then the Messiah would appear as the Prince.

Now we want to research the exact date on which Jesus did appear in Israel as *Prince* (since this is the emphasis in Daniel 9:25).

The Timing of the Entrance into Jerusalem

The Jewish people celebrated Jesus as their King and Messiah when He entered Jerusalem. He began His public ministry "during the 15th year of the reign of the

Emperor Tiberius" (Luke 3:1) who reigned from 14 to 37 AD. Thus the 15th year of his reign would have been 29 AD. Jesus' public mission lasted around three years. In John 2:13; 6:4; 11:55 three Passover feasts are mentioned at which Jesus participated. Luke 13:7 backed this directly and speaks of three years of His public activity.

John 12:1 says that Jesus came to Bethany six days before the Passover of the Jews (in 32 AD). Verses 12ff. report that His entry into Jerusalem, when He was fêted as Prince, took place the following day. According to the Jewish calendar, the fifth day before the start of the Feast of the Passover in 32 AD, occurred in the month of Nisan, (the Jews' Passover always took place in Nisan). Thus the commencement and termination of the 69 weeks of years are known: 445 BC (March/April) and 32 AD (March/April).

The Length of the 69 Weeks of Years

The prophetic year in the Bible lasts 360 days[23] (compare Revelation 11:3 with Revelation 12:14 where 3½ years are equated with 1260 days. Consequently one year has 360 days.). Therefore the 69 weeks of years has a total of 173,880 days (69 x 7 x 360). This time span would have to lie between the dates noted above. If we grasp the barely recognised fact that, in contrast to astronomy, there is no year 0 in history (1 BC is followed immediately by 1 AD), it is possible to ascertain that 173,880 days fit exactly between March/April 445 BC and March/April 32 AD. Daniel 9 has been fulfilled!

Deductions from this Prophecy

Amazingly the prophecy in Daniel 9 has been accurately fulfilled. This would be just *one* of over 330 prophecies! Of course, such exactitude always encounters scepticism. But with Daniel 9 the same mistake cannot be made as the Neo-Platonist Porphyry (300 AD) once did, who in the twelfth book of his *Against the Christians* declared the eleventh chapter of the prophet Daniel to be a forgery on the grounds that it contained too accurate a prophecy.

Historical Confirmation of Biblical Prophecy

If one wanted to cast doubt on the validity of the prophecy of Daniel 9, it would only be possible if the date of Jesus' appearance in Israel were wrong, since the passage itself, as well as the date of the decree to rebuild Jerusalem, is not open to question (cf. the Dead Sea Scrolls and the Septuagint translation). It follows clearly from several non-Biblical sources that Jesus lived and died during the reign of the Emperor Tiberius (14-37 AD), and that of the Roman Procurator Pilate (26-36 AD). Tacitus (55-c.115 AD), a respected Roman historian, reported about the Christians in Rome in his Annals (XV,44) and explained in this respect: "The name, Christian, has its origins in Jesus Christ, who was executed by Pontius Pilate under Tiberius."[24]

Flavius Josephus (37-100 AD) agreed, writing in his work "Anitiquitates Judaicae" that "At this time lived Jesus, a wise man........when Pilate sentenced him to the cross from the evidence of our leading men."[25]

Tertullian (2nd century AD) said in the Apologia 5,2: "Tiberius, in whose time the Christian name first made its appearance in the world …"[26]

From these witnesses it is clear that Jesus appeared in Israel between 26 and 36 AD. The 69 weeks of years fit in exactly from 445 BC up to the period of 26-36 AD. Even if we were to consider the possibility of a certain inaccuracy in counting the years, which I have referenced from the relevant literature, nevertheless it is clear that Daniel's weeks of years fit exactly into the time of Artaxerxes to Tiberius. Daniel 9 has been fulfilled!

Supplementary Comments
The Division of the Weeks of Years
It is quite justifiable to ask why the 69 weeks of years are divided up into 7 plus 62 weeks of years. This issue is resolved in the following way: The first 7 weeks of years (49 years) relates to the time it took for the complete rebuilding of the city of Jerusalem, about which Daniel 9:25 says:

"Know therefore and understand, that from the going forth of the commandment to restore and to build Jerusalem unto the Messiah the Prince shall be seven weeks, and threescore and two [62] weeks" (Daniel 9:25).

The further 62 weeks of years began immediately after the completion of the restoration Jerusalem.

This issue is very important! For then how could we know that the decree to rebuild and restore Jerusalem in Daniel 9 is the one from Artaxerxes, and not the one from Cyrus (Kores) in the year 539 BC (cf. Isaiah 44:28; Ezra 1)? Daniel 9 says: in the first 49 years after the decree - by which is meant here that the city of Jerusalem would undergo restoration. In contrast to Cyrus, this was the case only with Artaxerxes. So the Jew of the OT could clearly know that he should reckon the coming of the Messiah from the decree of 445 BC.

The Prediction of Daniel 9:26

According to Daniel 9:26, after the 69 weeks of years the Messiah would be "cut off (technically 'exterminated') and have nothing." What it doesn't say is how much time would elapse before this would happen. From the Gospels, however, we discover that Jesus was crucified exactly 5 days after His appearance as Prince.

Explanation of the Expression "The People of the Prince to Come"

This expression refers to the Romans who, after Jesus' crucifixion, destroyed the Temple and the entire city of Jerusalem. This event occurred in 70 AD.

An eye witness account can be found in the book "De bello Judaico" (= History of the Jewish War) written by Flavius Josephus. The prominent Rabbi Solomon Yarchi (1070-1105), known by the name Rashi, author of a commentary on 23 Talmud Tractates as well as that of the whole of the Bible (OT), said that the Daniel 9 prophecies here foretold the suffering which the Jewish people had to endure under the general Titus at the destruction of Jerusalem in the year 70 AD.[27] Other Jewish sources confirm this statement.[28]

Moshe Ben Maimon and Daniel 9

The Rabbi Moshe Ben M Maimon (= Moses Maimonides, 1135-1204), one of the greatest Jewish scholars of the Middle Ages, who was called "The Second Moses" due to his extraordinary influence on the theological thinking of Judaism, expressed himself very significantly regarding the calculation of the weeks of years in his letter: "iggereth hatheman":

"Inasmuch as Daniel has proclaimed the matter a deep secret, our sages have interdicted the calculation of the time of the future redemption, or the reckoning of the period of the advent of the Messiah, because the masses might be mystified and bewildered should the Messiah fail to appear as forecast. The rabbis invoked God to frustrate and destroy those who seek to determine precisely the advent of the messianic era, because they are a stumbling block to the people, and that is why they uttered the imprecation, "May the calculators of the final redemption come to grief." (Sanhedrin 97b).[29]

This statement requires no further comment; it is self-explanatory.

The Uniqueness of the Fulfilment

It has now become apparent how the coming of the Messiah was explicitly foretold in the OT and how these details have been fulfilled exactly in Jesus Christ. With this in mind, it is worth noting that more than 40 people have come forward claiming to be the promised Messiah within the entire span of Jewish history. Most of these people are not talked about today. Of all these false Messiahs Bar Kochba (132 AD), and Shabbetai Tzvi (1665 AD) attained the greatest significance, since they stirred up large parts of the Jewish world. Compared with the Promised One, it becomes quite clear that both of them came too late on the scene to be the promised Messiah, the one being around 100 years too late, the other some 1630 years. None of these false Messiahs could support his claim through fulfilled prophecy!

2. The "Shevet" of Judah

The patriarch Jacob (19th century BC) also gave a prophecy about the coming Messiah. Shortly before his death he proclaimed to his twelve sons, the fathers of the twelve tribes of Israel, just what would happen to their offspring (cf. Genesis 49:1-2). Jacob's statement regarding the tribe of Judah is of particular significance in connection with Messianic prophecy.

The sceptre shall not depart from Judah, nor a lawgiver from between his feet, until Shiloh come (= the one making peace, the one bringing peace*); and unto him shall the gathering of the people be"* [Genesis 49:10].

The Messianic Interpretation of Genesis 49:10 in Judaism

The expression "Shilo" is one of the many names of the Messiah in the OT. When, in the Talmud, Rabbi Yochanan (1st century AD) is asked for the name of the Messiah, the answer is given that his name is "Shilo."[30]

A Messianic understanding of this passage is likewise found in many other Rabbinic writings.[31] In particular I would like to mention two important documents: the Onkelos Targum,[32] and Bereshith Rabba (§98).[33]

The Meaning of the Word "Shevet"

The Hebrew word "shevet", which is translated here as "sceptre," denotes a "stick" or a "staff". From Numbers 17 it follows that each of the twelve tribes of Israel was in possession of a staff or sceptre bearing the name of the prince of the respective tribe. This staff was among other things a symbol of the *might* and *identity* of a tribe.[34]

The word "shevet" means both "sceptre" and "tribe" in Hebrew. From this it becomes clear: in a play on words in the Bible "shevet" symbolises the identity and power of an Israelite tribe.

Now the statement in Genesis 49:10 becomes clear: The identity and might of the tribe of Judah would not perish until the Messiah would come.

The National Collapse of Judah

When the Romans brought an end to the Jewish state in 70 AD, the national identity of the tribe of Judah collapsed. The political leadership also departed from Judah at that time. Consequently the Messiah must have come before this point in time. Jesus of Nazareth actually appeared in Israel some 40 years before!

Judah's Identity in Babylon

When looking at the Babylonian captivity of Judah, let it be noted that at that point the national identity of the tribe of Judah had not collapsed, since Judah, in the particular sense of a nation, was displaced geographically. From Ezekiel 8:1 and 20:1 we can see that Judah also possessed a political leadership at this time. From this time on the tribe was under foreign rule.

Chapter 2

The Messiah's Ancestry and Origin

1. His Family tree

Up until 70 AD it was possible, normally at least, for every Jew by birth to be able to trace his family tree, as 1 Chronicles 9:1 indicated that the whole of Israel was listed in genealogical lists. It was in one's own interests to have one's genealogy to hand, because anyone who wasn't able to prove his ancestry was deemed not to be a true Israelite, which had its disadvantages (Ezra 2:59-62; Nehemiah 7:61-65).

Anyone who was employed in public office, and was well-known for it, it was a matter of course that his genealogy, or at the very least some well-known ancestors from it, would then be made known to the public at large. Had the genealogy of someone who wanted to hold public office not been immaculate, then he would have been dismissed as incompetent.

These preliminary remarks are very important in connection with the fact that in the OT it was promised to certain people that the Messiah would be a direct descendant of theirs.

Genealogies from the Gospels of Matthew and Luke

We are given the genealogy of Joseph, Jesus' foster father, in Matthew 1, and that of Mary, the mother of Jesus, in Luke 3. The latter is of greatest importance for the further explanations.

Below is Mary's genealogy from Luke 3:23-38:[35]

"And Jesus himself began to be about thirty years of age, being (as was supposed) *the son of Joseph, which was the son of Heli (= Mary's father!), which was the son of Matthat, which was the son of Levi, which was the son of Melchi, which was the son of Janna, which was the son of Joseph, which was the son of Mattathias, which was the son of Amos, which was the son of Naum, which was the son of Esli, which was the son of Nagge, which was the son of Maath, which was the son of Mattathias, which was the son of Semei, which was the son of Joseph, which was the son of Juda, which was the son of Joanna, which was the son of Rhesa, which was the son of Zorobabel, which was the son of Salathiel, which was the son of Neri, which was the son of Melchi, which was the son of Addi, which was the son of Cosam, which was the son of Elmodam, which was the son of Er, which was the son of Jose, which was the son of Eliezer, which was the son of Jorim, which was the son of Matthat, which was the son of Levi, which was the son of Simeon, which was the son of Juda, which was the son of Joseph, which was the son of Jonan, which was the son of Eliakim, which was the son of Melea, which was the son of Menan, which was the son of Mattatha, which was the son of Nathan, which was the son of David, which was the son of Jesse, which was the son of Obed, which was the son of Booz, which was the son of Salmon, which was the son of Naasson, which was the son of Amminadab, which was the son of Aram,*

which was the son of Esrom, which was the son of Phares, which was the son of Juda, which was the son of Jacob, which was the son of Isaac, which was the son of Abraham, which was the son of Thara, which was the son of Nachor, which was the son of Saruch, which was the son of Ragau, which was the son of Phalec, which was the son of Heber, which was the son of Sala, which was the son of Cainan, which was the son of Arphaxad, which was the son of Sem, which was the son of Noe, which was the son of Lamech, which was the son of Mathusala, which was the son of Enoch, which was the son of Jared, which was the son of Maleleel, which was the son of Cainan, which was the son of Enos, which was the son of Seth, which was the son of Adam, which was the son of God."

God's Promises to Abraham, Isaac, and Jacob

In the 21st century BC God promised *Abraham* on several occasions that the Messiah would be one of his descendants. For example, it says in Genesis 22:18:

"... *And in thy seed* (= your descendant) *shall all nations of the earth be blessed; because thou hast obeyed my voice.*"

Here it doesn't say "and in your seeds", as in many descendants, but "in your seed". This descendant is the Messiah (Galatians 3:16).

In the 20th century BC God promised several times that the Messiah would be a descendant of *Isaac*. In Genesis 26:4, for example, God says to Isaac: "... *and in thy seed shall all the nations of the earth be blessed.*"

Likewise, around 1874 BC, *Jacob*, who later acquired the name Israel, was also given the promise that the Messiah would be his descendant: "... *and in thy seed shall all the families of the earth be blessed"* (Genesis 28:14). Thus in c. 1874 BC it was clearly revealed that the Messiah would be an Israelite. The question remains though – from which of the 12 tribes of Israel would the Messiah come?

The Messiah would be a descendant of the tribe of Judah

In the year 1804 BC, the patriarch Jacob declared to his twelve sons what would happen to their descendants. To his son Judah he said:

"The sceptre shall not depart from Judah, nor a lawgiver from between his feet, until Shiloh (= the one making peace, the one bringing peace*) come; and unto him shall the gathering of the people be"* (Genesis 49:10).

The Messiah would be a descendant of Judah, and not one from Rueben, Simeon, Levi, Zebulun, Issachar, Dan, Gad, Asher, Naphtali, Joseph or Benjamin. 1 Chronicles 5:2 (c. 530 BC) expresses the same fact with different words: *"For Judah prevailed above his brethren, and of him came the chief ruler."* Incidentally, the word for ruler (Hebrew "nagid") in this passage is the same word employed in Daniel 9:25.

But from which family in Judah would the Messiah come from ?

The Messiah would come from the Family of Jesse

The prophet Isaiah answered the question posed above in 11:11:

"And there shall come forth a rod out of the stem of Jesse, and a Branch shall grow out of his roots."

In the Targum of Jonathan Ben Uzziel[36] this Bible verse is understood as Messianic, the title "Messiah" being inserted there to explain it.

Isaiah prophesied that the Messiah would come from the family of Jesse, the Bethlehemite. Jesse had *eight sons* (cf. 1 Samuel 16), however, so which one of these would be the ancestor of the Messiah?

The Messiah would be a Descendant of David

The OT confirms this in several passages, that the Messiah would be a son of *David*, the son of Jesse. In 600 BC Jeremiah proclaimed:

"Behold, the days come, saith the LORD, that I will raise unto David a righteous Branch ... and [he] shall execute judgment and justice in the earth" (Jeremiah 23:5; cf. Jeremiah 33:15).

Also in Psalm 132:11 it is written: *"The LORD hath sworn in truth unto David; he will not turn from it; Of the fruit of thy body will I set upon thy throne."*

God had bound Himself by an oath to David that the Messiah would be a direct descendant of his (cf. also Psalm 89:35,36).

Confirmation from Mary's Genealogy

All the people named above are found in the genealogy of Mary, Jesus' mother, thus confirming that these prophecies have been fulfilled in the historic Jesus of Nazareth.

The ancestry of Jesus was generally well known among the Jewish people, hence calling Him "Son of David" (cf. Luke 18:38-39; Matthew 21:9,15,27; see also

Matthew 15:22). Had this all not been the case, the Jewish leaders of that time would have been able to use this as an argument against Jesus' claim to be the Messiah. Such an easily verifiable fact could not be denied or be questioned.

Luke, the Historian

Since Jesus' genealogy had been copied by Luke, let it be noted that archaeology was able to confirm Luke as an exact, precise and credible historian. After long years of research the famous archaeologist William Ramsay arrived at the conclusion that Luke's rendering of historical facts is unrivalled when it came to its credibility. Other archaeologists have carried on Ramsay's work, their results clearly showing that Luke's history is indeed absolutely reliable down to the smallest detail.[37]

Since Luke's Gospel is reliable to such an extent and credible, the other three Gospels of the NT, Matthew, Mark and John, are, too. They agree with Luke and therefore they are confirmed by Luke historically.

2. The Messiah's Birthplace

The Prophecy of Micah

During the 8th century BC, Micah of Moresheth acted as a prophet (cf. Micah 1:1). He was entrusted with declaring the birthplace of the Messiah. In Micah 5:2 God says:

"But thou, Bethlehem Ephrathah, though thou be little among the thousands of Judah, yet out of thee shall he

*come forth unto me that is to be ruler in Israel; whose go-
ings forth have been from old, from everlasting."*

There were two places in the land of Israel with the
name Bethlehem; the one in Galilee (cf. Joshua 19:15-
16), and the other in Judea. The latter was named Bethlehem Ephrathath in order to differentiate between the
two.

The Messiah would be born in this village, situated
about 10 km (c. 6 miles) south of Jerusalem, with probably less than 1,000 inhabitants at the time of Jesus. The
prophet Micah was able to predict this with such precision and certainty, many centuries before it came to
pass.

The New Testament Confirmation
It is confirmed in the NT that Jesus was indeed born in
Bethlehem Ephrathath. Matthew 2:1 says:

*"Now when Jesus was born in Bethlehem of Judæa in
the days of Herod the king ..."*

This was likewise confirmed by the doctor, Luke, in
the second chapter of his Gospel. Think again about
what was discussed in the section "Luke, the Historian"
concerning the credibility of the Gospels.

Micah 5:2 had always been understood well
When the Edomite, Herod the Great, heard that a new
King had been born, he gathered together all the leading
priests and scribes and demanded to know just where
the birthplace of the Messiah was. They answered:

*"In Bethlehem of Judæa, for thus it is written by the
prophet"* (Matthew 2:5).

The scribes weren't the only ones who understood this point, for John reported that this was also accepted by the common people, who said: *"Shall Christ (= Hebrew Messiah) come out of Galilee? Hath not the scripture said, That Christ cometh of the seed of David, and out of the town of Bethlehem, where David was?"* (John 7:41-42).

Further proof that Micah's prophecy was well understood comes from the Septuagint, in which this passage has been so well translated that we can conclude from it that the translator must have well understood what he had rendered into Greek.

Michah 5 in the Targum of Jonathan

The Targum of Jonathan Ben Uzziel on the Prophets[38] also clearly shows the Messianic interpretation of this passage in Judaism. The title "Messiah" is used there in the text for clarification purposes.

3. Jesus of Nazareth

Jesus is called a "Nazarene" or "of Nazareth" a total of 18 times in the NT. This name comes from the Hebrew word "nezer", which basically had the meaning "sapling", "shoot", or "branch".

Jesus was generally known as "Jesus of Nazareth" by the Jewish public between 29 and 32 AD. He was even called that by His greatest opponents (cf. John 18:5,7). This fulfilled what the prophets had declared, i.e. that the Messiah would be called a "sapling", or a "shoot"

Predictions by the Prophets Zechariah, Jeremiah, and Isaiah

The prophet Zechariah declared the following about the Messiah in 520 BC:

Thus speaketh the LORD of hosts ... "Behold the man whose name is The BRANCH" (Zechariah 6:12).

"... behold I will bring forth my servant the BRANCH" (Zechariah 3:8).

Both these passages are also identified as Messianic in the Targum of Jonathan!

About 80 years before Zechariah, Jeremiah declared: *"Behold, the days come, saith the LORD, that I will raise unto David a righteous Branch, ... and he shall execute judgment and justice in the earth"* (Jeremiah 23:5).

The prophet Isaiah also named the Messiah in this way: *"In that day shall the branch of the LORD be beautiful and glorious"* (Isaiah 4:2).

A Word-play in Hebrew

Although the Hebrew word "zemach" (= "sapling", "shoot" or "branch") was used in the passages mentioned, it was possible for any Jew well-versed in the Scriptures, when he heard of "Jesus of Nazareth", to connect the name "Nazarene/of Nazareth" with the word "zemach" in the passage under consideration. The meanings of names play a great role in the Bible!

There are further references to "Nazarene" in the OT. In Isaiah 11:1, for example, it says: *"And there shall come forth a rod out of the stem of Jesse, and a Branch shall grow out of his roots"* (Isaiah 11:1).

The word used for "shoot" in the original text of this passage is "nezer". This is the root of the name "Nazarene"!

A Justified Question

We would be justified in asking ourselves, why Jesus wasn't referred to as "Jesus of Bethlehem," as opposed to just "Jesus of Nazareth", given the fact that he was born in Bethlehem.

The following explanation should explain this issue: When the terrible and cruel King Herod the Great ordered the murder of the children (cf. Matthew 2), Joseph and Mary fled with the child from Bethlehem to Egypt. After the death of Herod they returned and wanted to settle back in Bethlehem. However, when Joseph heard that the cruellest of Herod the Great's sons, Archelaus,[39] had become the ruler over Judæa, he was afraid to go and settle there. This was with good reason: Actually Herod Antipas (the brother of Archelaus) should have succeeded Herod the Great, but his father altered his will in a fit of rage shortly before his death, granting Archelaus the throne instead.[40]

Hence Joseph and Mary travelled with the child to the region of Galilee and stayed in Nazareth, where Jesus spent the next 28 years. It was because of this that Jesus was known as "Jesus of Nazareth".

It is remarkable just how all the political circumstances at that time were involved in the fulfilment of these Messianic prophecies (cf. Psalm 79:10).

Even today critics still often refer to Jesus as "Jesus of Nazareth", so that the prophecy that the Messiah would be called a Nazarene is still confirmed by His opponents.

4. Out of Egypt

It seems rather paradoxical when we ascertain that God caused the prophet Hosea (in the 8th century BC) to proclaim that the Messiah would come *from Egypt*. In Hosea 11:1 it says:

".... and [I] called my son out of Egypt."

In Matthew 2 we can read the fulfilment of this prophecy. Mary and Joseph, who had fled to Egypt because of Herod the Great's order to kill the children, returned to Israel after the death of this tyrant. The Messiah actually came out of Egypt.

Now it is clear. The prophets have expressed themselves very precisely: the Messiah would be *born* in Bethlehem, be *named* "of Nazareth", and be *called* out of Egypt!

Chapter 3

The Public Appearance of the Messiah (29-32 AD)

1. His Forerunner

The Announcement by the Prophets Malachi and Isaiah

In the third chapter of Malachi, the voice of the Messiah is heard when he says:

"Behold, I will send my messenger, and he shall prepare the way before me: and the Lord, whom ye seek, shall suddenly come to his temple, even the messenger of the covenant, whom ye delight in: behold, he shall come, saith the Lord of hosts." (Malachi 3:1).

Shortly before the appearance of the Messiah in public, a prophet would arise with the commission to prepare the people for the coming of the Messiah in the very near future.

Isaiah also spoke of this forerunner, and named him "the voice of one calling in the wilderness". In Isaiah 40:3 it states:*"The voice of him that crieth in the wilderness, Prepare ye the way of the LORD, make straight in the desert a highway for our God."*[41]

Isaiah informs us that this forerunner would appear *in the desert.*

The Function of this Forerunner

This forerunner would have the important task of preparing the people of Israel for the imminent coming of the Messiah, so that they could readily accept Him. There should be nothing more in the hearts of the people that would be able to hinder accepting the promised Messiah; rather, their hearts should be "straight paths" (cf. Psalm 84:5). Therefore it is stated furthermore in Isaiah 40:4-5:

"Every valley shall be exalted and every mountain and hill brought low; the crooked places shall be made straight and the rough places smooth; the glory of the LORD shall be revealed, and all flesh shall see it together; For the mouth of the LORD has spoken."

The announcement of this forerunner has its complete fulfilment in John the Baptist, son of Zachariah. His appearance occurred in 29 AD, with Luke noting that this was during the 15th year of the reign of the Emperor Tiberius (Luke 3:1).

450 Years without Prophets

John the Baptist's appearance was sensational, there having arisen virtually no prophets of the LORD in Israel for some 450 years (the last prophet of the OT was Malachi). There is a lament concerning the dearth of prophets in Israel in a historical source from the inter-testamental period (spanning over 450 years). 1 Maccabees 9:27 states: "So there was a great affliction in Israel, the like whereof was not since the time that a prophet was not seen among them."

In the Babylonian edition of the Talmud it is reported that the Holy Spirit had departed from the land of

Israel after the prophets Haggai, Zachariah, and Malachi (BT Sanhedrin 11a).

It can be seen how great the sensation caused by John the Baptist's appearance was from the sheer number of people who came to him from Jerusalem, Judæa, and all the surrounding areas (Matthew 3:5).

John the Baptist at Work

John baptized in the desert and preached the baptism of repentance for the forgiveness of sins. With striking and rousing speech never before heard, he made it clear to the people of Israel that the Messiah would be coming very shortly, and everyone needed to repent by confessing their sins to the living God, showing remorse for them and making themselves ready to encounter the promised Messiah. He emphasised further that for those who wouldn't accept the Messiah and repent, it would be impossible to flee the wrath of God. The reader is advised to compare the Gospel reports of John the Baptist's appearance in the wilderness (Matthew 3; Mark 1; Luke 3; and John 1).

Jesus Appears

Matthew 3:13 reports that at the time when John baptized and preached, Jesus came to him to be baptized as well. This agrees again with Isaiah 40. Verse 5 states:

"And the glory of the LORD shall be revealed, and all flesh shall see it together: for the mouth of the LORD hath spoken it."

Jesus, the Messiah, the God of the OT become human, made His public appearance directly after the appearance of John the Baptist. It is in this context that Isaiah speaks about the appearance of the Lord Jesus as "The Revelation of the Glory of the Eternal One". It is interesting to read what an eye-witness had to say about this. The disciple, John, witnessed about the Lord Jesus:

"And the Word was made flesh, and dwelt among us, (and we beheld his glory, the glory as of the only begotten of the Father,) full of grace and truth" (John 1:14).

John the Baptist in the Writings of Josephus

The 1st-century historian, Flavius Josephus, confirms the historicity of John the Baptist in his work "Antiquities of the Jews" (XVIII,5.2).

2. The Public Ministry of the Messiah

Where the Messiah actually appeared

Should any one of the OT Israelites have wanted to know the actual geographical location where the Messiah was to begin His public ministry, they would need to refer to Isaiah 9:1-2 (0r 8:23-9:1):

"Nevertheless the dimness shall not be such as was in her vexation, when at the first he lightly afflicted the land of Zebulun and the land of Naphtali, and afterward did more grievously afflict her by the way of the sea, beyond Jordan, in Galilee of the nations. The people that walked in darkness have seen a great light: they that dwell in the land of the shadow of death, upon them hath the light shined."

The expression "a great Light" is a term for the light of the sun (cf. Genesis 1:16). Here this expression applies to the Messiah, Who is called "the sun of righteousness" in Malachi 4:2, and "the light of the world" in John 8:12. He would shine, like a rising sun, into the darkness of Israel. From Isaiah 9 we conclude that the inhabitants of Zebulun and Naphtali living by the Sea of Genezareth (= a region of Galilee) would be very honoured to be the first to see this Light.

From these observations on Isaiah 9:1-2 it is now clear that the Messiah would begin His public ministry in the region of Galilee.

Confirmation by the NT

In Matthew 4:12, 13 and 17 it states:

"Now when Jesus had heard that John was cast into prison, he departed into Galilee; and leaving Nazareth, he came and dwelt in Capernaum, which is upon the sea coast (i.e. by the Sea of Genezareth), in the borders of Zebulon and Nephthalim ... From that time Jesus began to preach, and to say, Repent: for the kingdom of heaven is at hand."

This very same fact is also confirmed in Luke 23:5 (cf. also Matthew 4:18-25).

The Messiah's Miracles

In several passages of the OT it is emphasised that miracles would be performed at the Messiah's appearance. In Isaiah 35:4-6 it states:

"Say to them that are of a fearful heart, Be strong, fear not: behold, your God will come with vengeance, even God with a recompence; he will come and save you. Then the

eyes of the blind shall be opened, and the ears of the deaf shall be unstopped. Then shall the lame man leap as an hart, and the tongue of the dumb sing: for in the wilderness shall waters break out, and streams in the desert."

A further miracle is prophesied in Isaiah 29:24: *"They also that erred in spirit shall come to understanding, and they that murmured shall learn doctrine."*

So the crippled, the blind, the deaf, the dumb, and those who had erred in spirit would be healed by the Messiah!

The Fulfilment of the Prophecies Confirmed by the NT

The NT confirms most clearly that these and yet other miracles were performed by the Lord Jesus. In John 9, for example, a blind man is healed, in Mark 2:3-12 a lame man, in Matthew 15:29-31 a mute and in Mark 7:31-37 a deaf man.

As far as the people who had erred in spirit are concerned, we might consider the lunatics of Matthew 4:24 who were, as were all other ill people, healed by the Lord Jesus.

The Miracles confirmed by the Talmud

In the Babylonian Talmud (BT Sanhedrin 43a) it is not in question that miracles were actually performed in Israel by the Lord Jesus. There it is spoken of in a blasphemous way, however, by calling the miracles magic (cf. Matthew 12:24).

The Witness of Justin Martyr

Further confirmation of miracles performed by Jesus Christ came from Justin Martyr (died c. 165 AD), who, in chapter 69 of his "Dialogue with Trypho the Jew", discusses the Jewish criticisms levelled at Jesus. He mentions that the Jews held Him to be a sorcerer ("magos"), and likewise of leading the people astray ("laoplanos").

The Witness of Origen
A further, somewhat identical piece of evidence is found in Origen (185-254 AD) who speaks about this in his work "Contra Celsum" (1,28). In this work Origen refers to an anti-Christian polemic paper written by a certain Celsus in c. 178 AD.

Psalm 72
The public ministry of the Messiah is spoken of in Psalm 72:12-13, as well as in many other OT passages. There it is written:

"For he shall deliver the needy when he crieth; the poor also, and him that hath no helper. He shall spare the poor and needy, and shall save the souls of the needy."

The Poor Man Crying for Help
In Luke 18:35-43 it says:

"And it came to pass, that as he was come nigh unto Jericho, a certain blind man sat by the way side begging: and hearing the multitude pass by, he asked what it meant. And they told him, that Jesus of Nazareth passeth by. And he cried, saying, Jesus, thou Son of David, have mercy on me. And they which went before rebuked him, that he should hold his peace: but he cried so much the more, Thou Son of David, have mercy on me. And Jesus stood, and commanded him to be brought unto him: and when he was come near, he asked him, saying, What wilt thou that I shall do unto thee? And he said, Lord, that I may receive

my sight. And Jesus said unto him, Receive thy sight: thy faith hath saved thee. And immediately he received his sight, and followed him, glorifying God: and all the people, when they saw it, gave praise unto God."

He who has no Helper

The cry of "him that hath no helper" is found in John 5, for example, where it speaks about a man who had been an invalid for 38 years in all, and who had to admit that he didn't have anyone to help him. This person was also healed by Jesus Christ.

Mercy on the Despised and the Poor

Luke 13:10ff. reports about the Messiah having pity on the poor – or the weak, as the Hebrew word in Psalm 72 can be translated. Having mercy on a poor person or a beggar is described in John 9 (see verse 8), for example.

The Prophet

We have concentrated so far on the *deeds* of the Messiah, but now we should briefly discuss the subject of what He said. Even Moses declared the Messiah to be a prophet.

Here we have the text of Deuteronomy 18:15,17-19:

"The Lord thy God will raise up unto thee a Prophet from the midst of thee, of thy brethren, like unto me; unto him ye shall hearken … and the Lord said unto me, They have well spoken that which they have spoken. I will raise them up a Prophet from among their brethren, like unto thee, and will put my words in his mouth; and he shall speak unto them all that I shall command him. And it

*shall come to pass, that whosoever will not hearken unto
my words which he shall speak in my name, I will require
it of him."*

The Fulfilment

Jesus showed Himself to be a Prophet by making predictions about the future, the fulfilment of which can
easily be proved.[42]

The Hebrew word for a prophet means not only one
who foretells the future, but also one who in general
declares what the will of (the) God is. This is important,
as we can deduce from Psalm 40:10 that the Messiah
would also proclaim the faithfulness, salvation, gener-
osity and the truth of God in Israel (= "the great assembly"). The fulfilment of this can be found detailed in the
Gospels (cf., for example, the Sermon on the Mount in
Matthew 5-7).

The question now, is how would the people of Israel
react to the Messiah?

3. How the people of Israel reacted
to their Messiah

One of the Greatest Paradoxes

The promised, and so eagerly-desired Messiah would be
completely rejected and hated by His own people! The
prophets were quite unanimous in foretelling this fact,
and it was actually fulfilled in the Lord Jesus Christ. In
Isaiah 49:7 the Messiah is spoken of as being "despised"
and "abhorred by the nation"! Incidentally, this verse
is interpreted as Messianic in the Babylonian Talmud
(Sanhedrin 97b)!

In Psalms 69:4 we hear the Messiah lamenting the hate which He encounters from His own people:[43]

"They that hate me without a cause are more than the hairs of mine head: they that would destroy me, being mine enemies wrongfully, are mighty: then I restored that which I took not away."

In Psalm 109:3-4 He says: *"They compassed me about also with words of hatred; and fought against me without a cause. For my love they are my adversaries: but I give myself unto prayer."*

The Contempt for the Messiah by the Jewish Leaders

In the book of Isaiah the contempt for the Messiah by the leaders of the Jewish nation is mentioned. In Isaiah 53:2-3 it states:

"For he shall grow up before him as a tender plant, and as a root out of a dry ground: he hath no form nor comeliness; and when we shall see him, there is no beauty that we should desire him. He is despised and rejected of men; a man of sorrows, and acquainted with grief: and we hid as it were our faces from him; he was despised, and we esteemed him not."

The Hebrew expression *ish*, which is translated here as "men", refers to elevated and powerful people![44] Here, the prophet had the leading authorities in Israel in mind.

Traps set for the Messiah

In Psalm 35:7 the Messiah says:

"For without a cause have they hid for me their net in a pit, which without cause they have digged for my soul."

Several times in the NT it is reported how traps were set for the Messiah by the leaders of Judaism, and how they desired to catch Him with questions (cf. Luke 11:53-54; Luke 14:1-5; Mark 12:13-17; see also Luke 6:7).

Plots to Murder the Messiah

In the Psalm 31:13 the Messiah complains of something worse :

"For I have heard the slander of many: fear was on every side: while they took counsel together against me, they devised to take away my life."

Mark describes the fulfilment: *"And the Pharisees went forth, and straightway took counsel with the Herodians against him, how they might destroy him (Jesus)"* (Mark 3:6).

John 11:53 likewise confirms the fulfilment of this Psalm.

The Rejection on 15th Nisan 32 AD

The Messiah would be completely rejected by both the masses of the common folk and their leaders. How strikingly was this total rejection expressed on the 15th Nisan, 32 AD, when Jesus the Messiah stood before Pontius Pilate:

"And Pilate, when he had called together the chief priests and the rulers and the people, said unto them, Ye have brought this man unto me, as one that perverteth the people: and, behold, I, having examined him before you, have found no fault in this man touching those things whereof ye accuse him: no, nor yet Herod: for I sent you to him; and, lo, nothing worthy of death is done unto him. I will therefore

chastise him, and release him. (For of necessity he must release one unto them at the feast.) *And they cried out all at once, saying, Away with this man, and release unto us Barabbas: (who for a certain sedition made in the city, and for murder, was cast into prison.) Pilate therefore, willing to release Jesus, spake again to them. But they cried, saying, Crucify him, crucify him. And he said unto them the third time, Why, what evil hath he done? I have found no cause of death in him: I will therefore chastise him, and let him go. And they were instant with loud voices, requiring that he might be crucified. And the voices of them and of the chief priests prevailed. And Pilate gave sentence that it should be as they required* " (Luke 23:13-24).

4. Judas Iscariot

In the previous section we discussed the enmity and hatred of the people of Israel towards the Messiah. However, in the OT there are several Bible verses in which *one* person especially among the people of Israel is spoken about who would hate the Messiah in a particular way. This prophesied person was completely fulfilled in Judas Iscariot, and is dealt with in the Psalms 41, 55, and 109, as well as in Zechariah 11.

Psalm 41

In verse 9 the Messiah speaks through the mouth of David:

"Yea, mine own familiar friend, in whom I trusted, which did eat of my bread, hath lifted up his heel against me."

The Friend and Confidante

This man would be a friend of the Messiah. Judas was indeed a friend during some three years when he was a disciple of the Lord Jesus (cf. the Gospels' reports, in particular Matthew 26:50 where he is expressly called "friend"). Of this man it is also reported that the Messiah *trusted* him. Was this not fulfilled in the fact that, of all the disciples, the Lord Jesus entrusted Judas with the money (cf. John 12:6; 13:29)?

The Messiah's Bread

This verse is rich in details! This enemy would eat the Messiah's bread. Before he would "lift up his heel against the Messiah", he would receive a sop from Him and eat it.

The fulfilment of this is found in John 13:21-30 where the Lord Jesus' last Passover with His disciples is described:

"*When Jesus had thus said, he was troubled in spirit, and testified, and said, Verily, verily, I say unto you, that one of you shall betray me. Then the disciples looked one on another, doubting of whom he spake. Now there was leaning on Jesus' bosom one of his disciples, whom Jesus loved. Simon Peter therefore beckoned to him, that he should ask who it should be of whom he spake. He then lying on Jesus' breast saith unto him, Lord, who is it? Jesus answered, He it is, to whom I shall give a sop, when I have dipped it. And when he had dipped the sop, he gave it to Judas Iscariot, the son of Simon. And after the sop Satan entered into him.*

Then said Jesus unto him, That thou doest, do quickly. Now no man at the table knew for what intent he spake this unto him. For some of them thought, because Judas had the bag, that Jesus had said unto him, Buy those things that we have need of against the feast; or, that he should give something to the poor. He then having received the sop went immediately out: and it was night."

Psalm 55

In Psalm 55:12-14 the Messiah says:

"For it was not an enemy that reproached me; then I could have borne it: neither was it he that hated me that did magnify himself against me; then I would have hid myself from him: but it was thou, a man mine equal, my guide, and mine acquaintance. We took sweet counsel together, and walked unto the house of God in company."

Trusted Company

In this passage the betrayer is also called "friend" by the Messiah. Again, here it is said that He trusted him. For some three years Judas Iscariot was, together with the other disciples, the trusted companion of the Lord Jesus and thus accurately fulfilled this Psalm.

Walking to the House of God

It follows from the Gospel records that Judas Iscariot frequently went to the temple with Jesus and the other disciples. A great crowd of people would often be there on such occasions. So they had many opportunities to hear the Lord Jesus preaching (cf., for example, Luke 19:47-21:38, particularly Luke 19:47-48 in connection with Luke 20:45)! Thus the "walking unto the house of God in company" was fulfilled literally.

Mocking

Furthermore, from this Psalm it follows that the Messiah's betrayer would *mock* Him. Doesn't this make us immediately think of the Judas kiss? Was this not a terrible mockery when he betrayed the Lord Jesus with a *kiss* (cf. Matthew 26:47-50)?

We often speak of the Judas kiss, but have you ever heard of the *Judas greeting*? In the Greek original of Matthew 26:49 it says that when Judas Iscariot betrayed Jesus with a kiss, he greeted him at the same time with the following words: "Chaire, rabbi".

Usually this salutation is translated simply as "hail, Rabbi". If the salutation is quite literally translated from the Greek, it is rendered as "be glad, Rabbi"!

Probably Judas said this in Aramaic with the words "shelam, rabbi". The salutation "shelam" means "peace, blessing, or good health". What a blasphemous, dastardly greeting this was in the face of the Lord Jesus Christ's imminent dreadful and cruel death on the cross!

The Thirty Pieces of Silver

In Zechariah 11 (c. 520 BC) it speaks of thirty pieces of silver for which Judas Iscariot betrayed the Lord Jesus. The Messiah speaks in verse 12:

"So they weighed for my price thirty pieces of silver."

The perfect fulfilment of this is found in Matthew 26:14-16:

"Then one of the twelve, called Judas Iscariot, went unto the chief priests, and said unto them, What will ye give me, and I will deliver him unto you? And they covenanted with him for thirty pieces of silver. And from that time he sought opportunity to betray him."

The Death of the Betrayer; his Office

After the betrayal Judas Iscariot committed suicide (Matthew 27:5). His end was prophesied in Psalm 109:8-9:

"Let his days be few; and let another take his office. Let his children be fatherless, and his wife a widow."

Which office did Judas Iscariot abandon that another would receive it? Luke 6:13-16 says that Judas had received the office of an apostle from the Lord Jesus. After Judas Iscariot's death this office went to a certain Matthias (cf. Acts 1:15-26).

Conclusion

Finally, it must be stated most clearly that Judas Iscariot was not predestined to betray Jesus. God, the Eternal One (YHWH), the One Who, as it was explained in the introduction, is not subject to the difference between past, present and future, *foreknew* that Judas Iscariot *of his own volition* and *on his own authority* would betray the Messiah, and He could therefore declare to the prophets this man's actions and desires many centuries before.

Chapter 4

The Judgement, Execution and Resurrection of the Messiah

1. The Judgement

The previous chapter drew our attention to the paradox of the people of Israel rejecting the promised Messiah. In the following chapter some of the prophecies are discussed which lay out in the clearest detail the climax of the rejection, namely His judgment and crucifixion, centuries before its fulfilment.

In Psalm 69:4 we hear His voice as He laments:

"They that hate me without a cause are more than the hairs of mine head: they that would destroy me, being mine enemies wrongfully, are mighty."

Also in Psalm 31:13 we find the Messiah's harrowing lament:

"For I have heard the slander of many: fear was on every side: while they took counsel together against me, they devised to take away my life" (cf. Mark 3:6 and John 11:53).

Being Led Away to Judgement

This hatred and rejection led to the Messiah, promised in the OT, being sentenced to death. In the well-known 53rd chapter of Isaiah it is described in the Prophetic Perfect Tense how He would be led away to judgement:

"He was oppressed, and he was afflicted, yet he opened not his mouth: he is brought as a lamb to the slaughter, and as a sheep before her shearers is dumb, so he openeth not his mouth" (Isaiah 53:7).

Isn't this described most clearly about the Lord Jesus in the Gospels? He willingly allowed Himself to be led away, and in no way did He put up any resistance. (cf. Matthew 26:47-75).

Unjust Witnesses

In Psalm 35:11-12, we hear the Messiah say:

"False witnesses did rise up … They rewarded me evil for good to the spoiling of my soul."

This is echoed in Psalm 38:14: *"Thus I was as a man that heareth not, and in whose mouth are no reproofs."*

We find the fulfilment of this prophecy in Matthew 26:59-62: *"Now the chief priests, and elders, and all the council, sought false witness against Jesus, to put him to death; but found none: yea, though many false witnesses came, yet found they none. At the last came two false witnesses, and said, This fellow said, I am able to destroy the temple of God, and to build it in three days. And the high priest arose, and said unto him, Answerest thou nothing? what is it which these witness against thee?"*

In this passage it comes especially clearly to the fore what hatred was borne against the Messiah. He would simply be killed, although He had only done good to the people and no-one could justly accuse Him.

Abuse

In Isaiah 50 we are told how the Messiah would be treated at this trial; he says:

"I gave my back to the smiters, and my cheeks to them that plucked off the hair: I hid not my face from shame and spitting" (Isaiah 50:6).

Matthew 26:66-67 describes its fulfilment:

"What think ye? They answered and said, He is guilty of death. Then did they spit in his face, and buffeted him; and others smote him with the palms of their hands."

Furthermore, the prophet Micah shares more details of the court proceedings:

"They shall smite the judge of Israel (i.e. the Messiah) *with a rod upon the cheek"* (Micah 5:1).

Matthew 27:30 describes its fulfilment:

"And they spit upon him, and took the reed, and smote him on the head."

Scourging

John 19:1 informs us:

"Then Pilate therefore took Jesus, and scourged him."

When we read this scourging scene we must be clear that Roman whips or scourges were leather thongs, fixed to a handle and with primarily sharp pieces of metal, stone or even barbs at their ends, which shredded the skin of the victim, turning his back into a mass of blood. In Psalm 129:3 the Messiah speaks prophetically of His scourging:

"The plowers plowed upon my back: they made long their furrows."

The Crown of Thorns

In Matthew 27:29 it states that a crown of thorns was placed on the Lord Jesus' head. These were thorns that were perhaps some 5-8 cm (2-3 inches)- long spikes. In dry condition they were hard and sharp, as sharp as a needle. Such a crown being put on anyone's head would have meant the skin being pierced in countless places on the head and forehead, causing great pain, with blood flowing everywhere, which would mat the hair and make it hang down messily. It proved a profoundly horrific sight! So now we can understand the words from Isaiah 52:14 where God witnessed about His Messiah hundreds of years beforehand:

"As many were astonied at thee; his visage was so marred more than any man, and his form more than the sons of men …"

2. The Crucifixion

Psalm 22

In this Psalm of David the crucifixion of the Messiah was described in minute detail, 1000 years before the events took place. Crucifixion itself was never practised by the Jews (criminals were usually stoned; cf., for example, Leviticus 20:2). Execution by crucifixion was practised in Israel especially by the Romans first; commonly only centuries after the writing of Psalm 22.

This Psalm was interpreted as Messianic by the Jews in the book Pesiqta Rabbati. The suffering there was understood to be atoning suffering(s)![45] Here is the text of the complete Psalm:

"To the chief Musician upon Aijeleth Shahar (hind of the morning), A Psalm of David.

(1) My God, my God, why hast thou forsaken me? why art thou so far from helping me, and from the words of my roaring? (2) O my God, I cry in the daytime, but thou hearest not; and in the night season, and am not silent. (3) But thou art holy, O thou that inhabitest the praises of Israel. (4) Our fathers trusted in thee: they trusted, and thou didst deliver them. (5) They cried unto thee, and were delivered: they trusted in thee, and were not confounded.

(6) But I am a worm, and no man; a reproach of men, and despised of the people.

(7) All they that see me laugh me to scorn: they shoot out the lip, they shake the head, saying, (8) He trusted on the Lord that he would deliver him: let him deliver him, seeing he delighted in him.

(9) But thou art he that took me out of the womb: thou didst make me hope when I was upon my mother's breasts. (10) I was cast upon thee from the womb: thou art my God from my mother's belly. (11) Be not far from me; for trouble is near; for there is none to help. (12) Many bulls have compassed me: strong bulls of Bashan have beset me round. (13) They gaped upon me with their mouths, as a ravening and a roaring lion. (14) I am poured out like water, and all my bones are out of joint: my heart is like wax; it is melted in the midst of my bowels. (15) My strength is dried up like a potsherd; and my tongue cleaveth to my jaws; and thou hast brought me into the dust of death.

(16) For dogs have compassed me: the assembly of the

wicked have inclosed me: they pierced my hands and my feet. (17) I may tell all my bones: they look and stare upon me. (18) They part my garments among them, and cast lots upon my vesture.

(19) But be not thou far from me, O Lord: O my strength, haste thee to help me. (20) Deliver my soul from the sword; my darling from the power of the dog. (21) Save me from the lion's mouth: for thou hast heard me from the horns of the unicorns.

(22) I will declare thy name unto my brethren: in the midst of the congregation will I praise thee. (23) Ye that fear the Lord, praise him; all ye the seed of Jacob, glorify him; and fear him, all ye the seed of Israel.

(24) For he hath not despised nor abhorred the afflic-tion of the afflicted; neither hath he hid his face from him; but when he cried unto him, he heard. (25) My praise shall be of thee in the great congregation: I will pay my vows before them that fear him.

(26) The meek shall eat and be satisfied: they shall praise the Lord that seek him: your heart shall live for ever. (27) All the ends of the world shall remember and turn unto the Lord: and all the kindreds of the nations shall worship before thee. (28) For the kingdom is the Lord's: and he is the governor among the nations. (29) All they that be fat upon earth shall eat and worship: all they that go down to the dust shall bow before him: and none can keep alive his own soul.

(30) A seed shall serve him; it shall be accounted to the Lord for a generation. (31) They shall come, and shall declare his righteousness unto a people that shall be born, that he hath done this."

Pierced Hands and Feet

In verse 16 the Messiah says:

"For dogs have compassed me: the assembly of the wicked have inclosed me: they pierced my hands and my feet."

The expression "dogs" was used to describe non-Jews (cf. Matthew 15:21-28).[46] It had to be a non-Jewish squad, a Gentile band who would pierce His hands and feet,[47] i.e. who would crucify him.

Matthew 27:27-31 clearly confirms this fact:

"Then the soldiers of the governor took Jesus into the common hall, and gathered unto him the whole band of soldiers. And they stripped him, and put on him a scarlet robe. And when they had platted a crown of thorns, they put it upon his head, and a reed in his right hand: and they bowed the knee before him, and mocked him, saying, Hail, King of the Jews! (30) And they spit upon him, and took the reed, and smote him on the head. (31) And after that they had mocked him, they took the robe off from him, and put his own raiment on him, and led him away to crucify him."

Garments Divided and Wagered On

In the 18th verse it says that these Gentiles would firstly share out the Messiah's garments and, secondly, cast lots for His robe. How fittingly these details were also fulfilled:

"Then the soldiers, when they had crucified Jesus, took his garments, and made four parts, to every soldier a part; and also his coat: now the coat was without seam, woven from the top throughout. They said therefore among themselves, Let us not rend it, but cast lots for it, whose it shall be: that the scripture might be fulfilled, which saith, They

parted my raiment among them, and for my vesture they did cast lots. These things therefore the soldiers did" (John 19:23-24).

Bones out of Joint
In verses 14 the Messiah says: "All my bones are out of joint."

What awful and harrowing words! The limbs which now hung on the nails in His hands and feet were dislocated by the Crucified One's own weight!

Sweat and Thirst
The suffering Messiah's great distress, sweat and thirst under indescribable pain are expressed in verses 14 and 15: *"I am poured out like water, … My strength is dried up like a potsherd; and my tongue cleaveth to my jaws."*

Light and Darkness
In verse 2 the alternating periods of light and darkness are spoken of: *"O my God, I cry in the daytime, but thou hearest not; and in the night season, and am not silent."*

Mark 15:25 and 33 shows us its fulfilment: "And it was the third hour, and they crucified him … And when the sixth hour was come, there was darkness over the whole land until the ninth hour."

This darkness is also spoken of in Isaiah 50 (and likewise in Psalm 88:1). In Isaiah 50:3 God says, closely concerning the abuse of the Messiah:

"I clothe the heavens with blackness, and I make sackcloth their covering."

Confirmation of the Darkness by Thallus

This three-hour-long darkness on the day of the crucifixion of the Lord Jesus is also confirmed by extra-Biblical sources. The Samaritan historian, Thallus, who wrote in Rome in 52 A.D, spoke of it in his now lost "Histories". However, a fragment of it appears in Julius Africanus in the early 3rd century AD. There he says: "Thallus, in Book Three of his *History*, explains away the darkness as an eclipse of the sun – unreasonably, as it seems to me."[48]

This objection by Julius Africanus is significant, because there couldn't possibly have been an eclipse of the sun at that time – first of all because no eclipse of the sun could produce three hours of complete darkness; and secondly, at the time of the full moon (the crucifixion took place on the 15th of Nisan, 32 AD, at the middle of the month was a full moon) a total solar eclipse is impossible. It must have been a miracle which the prophets foretold most accurately and can be supported optimally by historical sources.

Scorn and Dishonour

In verses 6-8 of Psalm 22 the Messiah speaks about how He is scorned and despised by everyone:

"But I am a worm, and no man; a reproach of men, and despised of the people. All they that see me laugh me to scorn: they shoot out the lip, they shake the head, saying, He trusted on the LORD that he would deliver him: let him deliver him, seeing he delighted in him."

The NT shows how this was fulfilled in Matthew 27:39-44:

"And they that passed by reviled him, wagging their heads, and saying, Thou that destroyest the temple, and buildest it in three days, save thyself. If thou be the Son of

God, come down from the cross. Likewise also the chief priests mocking him, with the scribes and elders, said, He saved others; himself he cannot save. If he be the King of Israel, let him now come down from the cross, and we will believe him. He trusted in God; let him deliver him now, if he will have him: for he said, I am the Son of God. The thieves also, which were crucified with him, cast the same in his teeth."

Counted with the Transgressors; His earnest Intercession

Isaiah 53:12 speaks about the two criminals who were crucified with Jesus, as well as His earnest intercession for His oppressors:

"… because he hath poured out his soul unto death: and he was numbered with the transgressors (or criminals); and he bare the sin of many, and made intercession for the transgressors."

We can compare this to Luke 23:32-34: "And there were also two other, malefactors, led with him to be put to death. And when they were come to the place, which is called Calvary, there they crucified him, and the malefactors, one on the right hand, and the other on the left. Then said Jesus, Father, forgive them; for they know not what they do."

Gall and Vinegar

A further detail of the crucifixion is found in Psalm 69:21 where the crucified One Himself says:

"They gave me also gall [or poison] for my meat [or food]; and in my thirst they gave me vinegar to drink."

This passage predicts two details: 1. The Messiah would be offered poison. 2. Vinegar would be given Him for His thirst.

The fulfilment of these, how He was offered an anaesthetic in order to deaden the unbearable pain somewhat, is found in Matthew 27:32-35. The Roman soldiers wanted to administer this to Him, but He rejected it because He wanted to endure death on the cross fully conscious:

"And as they came out, they found a man of Cyrene, Simon by name: him they compelled to bear his cross. And when they were come unto a place called Golgotha, that is to say, a place of a skull, they gave him vinegar to drink mingled with gall: and when he had tasted thereof, he would not drink. And they crucified him, …"

The Greek term "chole", translated by "gall" in the passage above, denotes a pain-relieving drug as a painkiller which the Roman soldiers "mercifully" offered to certain people being crucified.

The description of fulfilment, how the Messiah was given vinegar to drink, is found in Matthew 27:45-48:

"Now from the sixth hour there was darkness over all the land unto the ninth hour. And about the ninth hour Jesus cried with a loud voice, saying, Eli, Eli, lama sabachthani? that is to say, My God, my God, why hast thou forsaken me? Some of them that stood there, when they heard that, said, This man calleth for Elias. And straightway one of them ran, and took a spunge, and filled it with vinegar, and put it on a reed, and gave him to drink."

Death

The conclusion to all this unfathomable suffering is mentioned in Psalm 22:15 where the Messiah prays to

His God: *"Thou hast brought me into the dust of death."*

The last word of the Crucified One is found in Psalm 31:5: *"Into thine hand I commit my spirit."*

The fulfilment of this can be read in Luke 23:46:

"And when Jesus had cried with a loud voice, he said, Father, into thy hands I commend my spirit: and having said thus, he gave up the ghost."

In a Rich Man's Grave

An important Messianic prophecy is found in Isaiah 53:9 where it says:

"And he made his grave with the wicked, and with the rich in his death; because he had done no violence, neither was any deceit in his mouth."

Criminals were often cremated in the fires of Topheth in the Valley of Hinnom, west of Jerusalem. This would have been "the grave of the wicked". From the passage above it follows that God would not have permitted any such ignominy, after the Messiah's death, and that the Messiah would get a rich man's grave. The fulfilment of this prophecy is reported in Matthew 27:57-60:

"When the even was come, there came a rich man of Arimathæa, named Joseph, who also himself was Jesus' disciple: he went to Pilate, and begged the body of Jesus. Then Pilate commanded the body to be delivered. And when Joseph had taken the body, he wrapped it in a clean linen cloth, and laid it in his own new tomb, which he had hewn out in the rock: and he rolled a great stone to the door of the sepulchre, and departed."

In the Hebrew text the word "death" in Isaiah 53:9 is actually plural, expressing the agony of this type of death.[49]

The Messiah's Length of Life

Did the OT hint at just how old the Messiah would be at His death? In Psalm 102, another Messianic Psalm, the Messiah cries to His God in prayer about the fact that He would die "in the midst of His days":

"O my God, take me not away in the midst of my days" (Psalm 102:24*)!*

The expression "in the midst of my days" is easy to understand once we know Psalm 90, which defines the short lifespan of humans on Earth. Verse 10 says: *"The days of our years are three-score years and ten [70 years] … yet is their strength labour and sorrow; for it is soon cut off, and we fly away."*

If the average life expectancy of an Israelite at the time of the OT was 70 years, it becomes clear what the expression "the midst of my days" would amount to. The Lord Jesus also fulfilled this prophecy, since He died at about the age of 33. He began His public ministry when He was about 30 years-old (Luke 3:23) and was at work for some three years until His death on the cross.

Not One Bone Broken

A somewhat strange-looking prediction about the Messiah is found in Psalm 34:20:

"He (the Eternal One*) keepeth all his bones: not one of them is broken."*

Comparing this prophecy with its fulfilment, all becomes clear. In John 19:31-33 it says:

"The Jews therefore, because it was the preparation, that the bodies should not remain upon the cross on the sabbath day, (for that sabbath day was an high day,*) besought Pilate that their legs might be broken, and that they might*

be taken away. Then came the soldiers, and brake the legs[50] of the first, and of the other which was crucified with him. But when they came to Jesus, and saw that he was dead already, they brake not his legs."

The Geographical Location of His Death

The place where the Messiah would die had been known of since the time of Abraham (c. 2000 BC).

In Genesis 22:1-19, we read the story of the offering of Isaac. This took place on one of the mountains in the Land of Moriah (Hebrew "eretz ha-moriyah", cf. Genesis 22:2).

Moriah is the Temple Mount in Jerusalem (cf. 2 Chronicles 3:1). The "Land ha-Moriyah" is simply an area around Jerusalem. Isaac was not put to death there, since he, as the son of Abraham, was simply a type, an illustrative reference to the Messiah. The actual site of the offering (it wasn't actually on Mount Moriah itself, but a mountain in the vicinity!) was given the name "YHWH yir'eh" (= "the Eternal One will designate Himself", cf. v.14 and vv.7b-8) by Abraham. This means that on this mountain God would see the true sacrifice to which this account points typologically (as a model). Genesis 22:14b says therefore:

"... as it is said to this day, In the mount of the LORD it shall be seen."

The Lord Jesus actually died in the Land of Moriah, outside the then city city walls of Jerusalem on the hill of Golgotha (cf. John 19:17-18; Hebrews 13:12)! So He fulfilled this prophecy, too!

The Significance of the Messiah's Suffering and Death

In order to offer an explanation for the suffering and death of the Messiah, we have to dig deeper into the Scriptures. The Bible shows in many passages from the OT (e.g. Psalm 14) and the NT that all people without exception have sinned. Romans 3:22b-23 states:

"For there is no difference: for all have sinned, and come short of the glory of God."

However, God is a completely holy and just God (Joshua 24:19; Psalm 7:11), and cannot tolerate or overlook sin, i.e. everything that contradicts His thoughts and His nature (cf. Habakkuk 1:13). Therefore He would have to condemn every human being. However, the Bible also states that God is love (1 John 4:8) and therefore He doesn't want to do this. He *"will have all men to be saved,"* says 1 Timothy 2:4!

So it was necessary for the Lord to find a solution in order to be able to offer humans forgiveness of sins and eternal salvation on the basis of His holiness and righteousness. This was only possible if a perfect, sinless and holy man were to suffer God's judgement as a substitute. Therefore God sent His own Son and had Him become human. The Scripture explicitly says that the Lord Jesus never committed any sin (1 Peter 2:22), and He is named as "the righteous one" seven times in the NT. When the Lord Jesus was hanging on the cross, God placed upon Him the sins of all those who believed in Him and also the sins of those who would do so in the future. Indeed, during the three hours of darkness God identified the Lord Jesus with every one of these sins and brought His wrath on Him (1 Peter 2:24; 2 Corinthians 5:21; Isaiah 53:10). During those three hours

God turned His back completely on the Messiah, and therefore the Crucified One had to utter the awful cry "*My God, my God, why hast thou forsaken me?*" (Psalm 22:1; Matthew 27:46). Then He died (Matthew 27:50). The redeeming work has been completed (John 19:30)! Now God can completely forgive every sinner who puts his trust in the Lord Jesus in remorse and repentance and confesses his sins to Him (1 John 1:9) on the basis of His blood that was shed on the cross at Golgotha. (Ephesians 1:7). In fact, Hebrews 9:22 indicates that forgiveness is not possible without the shedding of blood. Thus the words of Isaiah 53:6-8 have been fulfilled:

"He is despised and rejected of men; a man of sorrows, and acquainted with grief: and we hid as it were our faces from him; he was despised, and we esteemed him not. Surely he hath borne our griefs, and carried our sorrows: yet we did esteem him stricken, smitten of God, and afflicted. But he was wounded for our transgressions, he was bruised for our iniquities: the chastisement of our peace was upon him; and with his stripes we are healed. All we like sheep have gone astray; we have turned every one to his own way; and the LORD hath laid on him the iniquity of us all."

3. Observations on Isaiah 53

Given the fact that Isaiah 53 occupies such an important place in the Messianic prophecy, this passage will be dealt with in more detail separately. The section of Isaiah chapters 52:13-53:12 can rightly be described as "The Gospel of Isaiah". 700 years before Christ the Eternal One declared that the "Hope of Israel", the long-awaited Messiah, would be inexplicably despised and rejected by His own people. This "Gospel" also shows, however, that the Messiah would not just endure the suffering inflicted upon Him by man; no, He would also suffer at God's hand, dying as the righteous substitute for the unrighteous. What was the purpose of this? To save them from their sins!

The Authenticity of Isaiah
In order to bring home the credibility and authenticity of the prophecies of the prophet Isaiah again, let's remind ourselves of the remarks concerning the Septuagint and the complete scroll of Isaiah from Qumran made in the introduction. Isaiah 53 is fully preserved in both these written records!

The Jewish Re-interpretation of Isaiah 53
Judaism today has turned away completely from the Messianic interpretation of this passage from Isaiah. As the Rabbinic writings show, however, this was not originally the case! The most prevalent modern interpretation claims that the "servant of the LORD" is not the Messiah, but the people of Israel, or a part of them is. Suffering is to come upon the people of Israel, just as it is described here. However, this understanding of Isaiah 53 simply cannot be substantiated for various reasons with regards to content:

– When have the people of Israel, or a part of them, suffered for the sins of others (Isaiah 53:4,5,6,8,10,11,12)? Not even righteous men such as Noah, Daniel, and Job could have been able to do this according to Ezekiel 14:12-20!

- Can it be said of any Jew, besides the Messiah, that "because he had done no violence [wrong], neither was any deceit in his mouth" (Isaiah 53:9)?
- When have the people of Israel ever been buried in a rich man's grave, instead of a grave for the unrighteous (Isaiah 53:9)?
- According to verse 8 of this passage, the "Servant of the LORD" would die as a substitute for the people of Israel. So how can He be identical to the people, when here He is clearly distinguished from them?

How the Messiah was understood in Rabbinic Literature

As we have said, there is a series of passages in Rabbinic literature that apply Isaiah 53 to the Messiah. So, for example, the Babylonian Talmud (Sandrehin 98b), in the Book Pesikta Rabbati, Pisqua 37 (700 AD),[51] in the book of Midrash Ruth Rabbah on Ruth 2:12,[52] and in the commentary on Isaiah 52-53 written by Abrabanel.[53] In his text Abrabanel points out that all the ancient Jewish commentaries recognised the Messianic sense of this passage.

The Rabbi Alschech (16th century AD) said of Isaiah 53 "Our ancient Rabbis have accepted the witness of tradition, that King Messiah is spoken of here. From this we also conclude, following them, that the subject of this prediction must be held to be David, that is the Messiah, as this is obvious."[54]

In the Midrash Tanchuma (9th century AD?) the interpretation for the text *"Behold, my servant shall deal prudently"* runs as follows: "This is the King Messiah, who is high and exalted and most sublime, more sublime than Abraham, exalted above Moses, and higher than the ministering angels."[55]

In the Targum from Jonathan Ben Uzziel, the Aramaic re-writing of the prophets, found in a tradition going back to the pre-Christian era, the title "Messiah" is added to the sentence "Behold, my servant shall deal prudently" (Isaiah 52:13![56] We could continue to give yet further interesting evidence; however, we now need to concentrate on how these prophecies, which are written in the "Prophetic Perfect Tense" (cf. the Introduction), were fulfilled in the historic Jesus of Nazareth.

Observations on Isaiah 52:13-53:12

Isaiah 52:13: *"Behold, my servant shall deal prudently, he shall be exalted and extolled, and be very high."*

Before the awful suffering of the Messiah is described, His triumph is introduced first. The Messiah would be raised (from His grave; Acts 2:24), and lifted up (to heaven at the Ascension; Acts 1:9), and be very high (on the throne at the right hand of God; Mark 16:9).

Isaiah 52:14: *"As many were astonied at thee; his visage was so marred more than any man, and his form more than the sons of men."*

This verse describes how the Messiah was mistreated by people: His back was turned into a bloody mess, with His skin torn into strips when Pilate had Him scourged (with leather straps, at the end of which were most probably sharp metal pieces, stones or hooks; John 19:1). A crown of thorns was placed upon His head, the length of each being 5-8 cm (2-3 inches), so that His blood would run down into His hair over His face (John 19:2).

Isaiah 52:15: *"So shall he sprinkle many nations; the kings shall shut their mouths at him: for that which had not been told them shall they see; and that which they had not heard shall they consider."*

Later the message about the abused Messiah Jesus would be announced well beyond the borders of Israel into the world at large, where it caused a great sensation (cf. Romans 15:18-21). Even kings like Agrippa would hear about it (Acts 26:27-28), as well as the Emperor of Rome (Acts 25:11-12).

Isaiah 53:1: *"Who hath believed our report? and to whom is the arm of the Lord revealed?"*

Although the message of the Messiah and His suffering would be told out to the whole world, it encountered great unbelief. Only a relatively small proportion of the Jews would believe (John 12:37-38). However, the Gospel encountered (and still encounters) a great deal of rejection among the Gentiles, the non-Jews.

Isaiah 53:2a: *"For he shall grow up before him as a tender plant, and as a root out of a dry ground ..."*

This verse refers to the Messiah's growing up as a small child (the Hebrew word "yoneq" [= "twig"] also means "suckling"!). However, the Lord Jesus grew up "before Him", i.e. in perfect fellowship with His God (Luke 2:40-52). He grew up among a people characterised by hard-heartedness, unbelief and dead religiosity, precisely "out of dry ground".

Isaiah 53:2b-3: *"... he hath no form nor comeliness; and*

when we shall see him, there is no beauty that we should desire him. He is despised and rejected of men; a man of sorrows, and acquainted with grief: and we hid as it were our faces from him; he was despised, and we esteemed him not."

The expectation among the Jews regarding the Messiah was for a freedom fighter, destined to throw off the yoke of the Romans. Therefore the Messiah, who came as a humble "servant of the LORD", was shown contempt and dishonour, especially from the leading Jews, who rejected Him (the Hebrew word "ishim" denotes the highest rank among the people).

There were only a handful who recognised His glory, *"(... the glory as of the only begotten of the Father,) full of grace and truth"* (John 1:14).

Isaiah 53:4a: *"Surely he hath borne our griefs, and carried our sorrows ..."*

The Lord Jesus shared deeply in the sufferings of the many sick in Israel and carried them in His soul during His life on earth (Matthew 8:16-17; cf. John 11:33-36). Let's note that this verse refers to "grief" and "sorrow" rather than to "transgressions" and "iniquities"!

Isaiah 53:4b-6: *"... yet we did esteem him stricken, smitten of God, and afflicted. But he was wounded for our transgressions, he was bruised for our iniquities: the chastisement of our peace was upon him; and with his stripes we are healed. All we like sheep have gone astray; we have turned every one to his own way; and the LORD hath laid on him the iniquity of us all."*

It was one thing that Messiah Jesus suffered because of the wickedness of the Romans and the Jews (and this couldn't atone for one single sin!), but this verse refers to God punishing Him as a substitute on the cross during the three hours of darkness for all the sins of those who have confessed their sins in repentance to God (or who will repent), and trusted in the atoning sacrifice of the Messiah at Golgotha (or will have trusted; 1 John 1:9; Romans 3:23-26).

Isaiah 53:7: *"He was oppressed, and he was afflicted, yet he opened not his mouth: he is brought as a lamb to the slaughter, and as a sheep before her shearers is dumb, so he openeth not his mouth."*

The Lord Jesus endured all the punishment inflicted upon Him without offering any resistance. How splendidly this was fulfilled that "He opened not His mouth like a lamb" (Matthew 26:62; 27:12-14, etc)!

In the OT animals were brought to God as sacrifices for sin; it is remarkable that we can recognise from this passage in Isaiah, for example, how plain it was, even at that time, that these sacrifices were patterns for the real sin-removing sacrifice of the Messiah!

Isaiah 53:8: *"He was taken from prison and from judgment: and who shall declare his generation? for he was cut off out of the land of the living: for the transgression of my people was he stricken."*

The judgement of the Lord Jesus was by a corrupt kangaroo court which was executed in scandalous, hurried proceedings. The Sanhedrin had the duty to at least summon those who could have said something in defence of the accused when it came to "capital cases". Where were Jesus' defenders? It was precisely in haste that He was dragged through the court proceedings. Who can describe the depravity of that generation? They murdered their Messiah! But at the same time He died for the sake of the entire people of Israel (cf. Matthew 1:21; John 11:50-51).

Isaiah 53:9: *"And he made his grave with the wicked, and with the rich in his death; because he had done no violence, neither was any deceit in his mouth."*

The "grave with the wicked" would have been situated in the valley of Hinnom outside the city of Jerusalem, in the "rubbish incinerator". However, God did not allow any further disgrace. Thus, He was laid to rest in the tomb of the rich man, Joseph of Arimathea (Matthew 27:57-60). Jesus' innocence was confirmed three times by the witness of the apostles:

– *He knew of no sin* (2 Corinthians 5:21: Paul)
– *He committed no sin* (1 Peter 2:22; Peter)
– *There is no sin in Him* (1 John 3:5; John)

Isaiah 53:10: *"Yet it pleased the LORD to bruise him; he hath put him to grief: when thou shalt make his soul an offering for sin, he shall see his seed, he shall prolong his days, and the pleasure of the LORD shall prosper in his hand."*

While the Lord Jesus was hanging on the cross for the three hours of darkness, laden with guilt that was foreign to Him, the holy and righteous God had to abandon Him (Matthew 27:46) and smite Him as an substitute. However, once He had completed this redeeming work, the LORD "prolonged His days" raising Him from the dead on the third day. (Acts 1:3; 10:40-41; Romans 6:9; Revelation 1:18, etc.).

Isaiah 53:11: *"He shall see of the travail of his soul, and shall be satisfied: by his knowledge shall my righteous servant justify many (i.e. help them get righteousness); for he shall bear their iniquities."*

His redeeming work has consequences: People are released from their sin, being the "fruit of the suffering of His soul". Through Him all believers will be justified before God (Romans 3:26).

Isaiah 53:12: *"Therefore will I divide him a portion with the great, and he shall divide the spoil with the strong; because he hath poured out his soul unto death: and he was numbered with the transgressors; and he bare the sin of many, and made intercession for the transgressors."*

The Lord gave up His life freely (poured out in death; John 10:17-18), and was counted with the "transgressors" (Hebrew "posh'im" = "criminal", "rebel"; Luke 23:33) Therefore God will give Him the Messianic kingdom as His reward for this (Revelation 20:6), and the believing remnant of Israel will have a part in it (= "the strong"). Jesus interceded on the cross for those who are unworthy (Luke 23:34). He was a ransom for many, but not for all (cf. Hebrews 9:28; Mark 10:45)! Everyone who does not confess their sin to God, and therefore does not thank Him for the sacrifice of His Messiah Jesus, will themselves come under the eternal judgement of God (Matthew 25:41,46). But now is the day of salvation, and everyone who comes to the Lord Jesus will be accepted (Matthew 11:28-30; John 6:37)!

4. The Resurrection
The resurrection of the Messiah was also foretold in the OT! In Psalm 16:8-10 the Messiah Himself says:

"I have set the LORD always before me: because he is at my right hand, I shall not be moved. Therefore my heart is glad, and my glory rejoiceth: my flesh also shall rest in hope. For thou wilt not leave my soul in hell (she'ol = the realm of the dead*); neither wilt thou suffer thine Holy One to see corruption"*

This Bible verse cannot possibly have been referring to David, the writer of this psalm, since he had died 1000 years before the Messiah's life on Earth, and "saw", consequently, "corruption". Also, one could still see his grave in 32 AD in Jerusalem (cf. Acts 2:29)! We have testimony of the utmost clarity concerning the Lord Jesus, however, that He rose again three days after His death, and did not "see corruption" (cf. Matthew 28; Mark 16; Luke 24; John 20 and 21).

Over 500 Witnesses

There was a total of over 500 witnesses of the Resurrection (cf. 1 Corinthians 15:3-9). It is impossible to write these people off as deceivers, since untruthfulness is fundamentally contrary to the teaching of the NT to which they held fast most resolutely, and even to the extent that some of them were willing to lay down their lives as martyrs for their faith!

No Resurrection – No Christianity

The following fact is worthy of note: Around 57 AD the apostle Paul wrote in a letter to Corinth that the certainty of the Christian faith depended on the fact of the resurrection, i.e. if the Resurrection of the Lord Jesus were not historical fact, then the Christian faith would be over. In 1 Corinthians 15:16-19 it actually says:

"For if the dead rise not, then is not Christ raised: and if Christ be not raised, your faith is vain; ye are yet in your sins. Then they also which are fallen asleep in Christ are perished. If in this life only we have hope in Christ, we are of all men most miserable."

If the witnesses of the Resurrection had been deceivers, how then could they have made their whole proclamation dependent on a lie? The resurrection must be, therefore, an unshakeable certainty. That's why Paul writes in the following verse (1 Corinthians 15:20): *"But now is Christ risen from the dead, and become the first-fruits of them that slept."*

The Significance of the Resurrection

Christ's Resurrection from the dead is therefore of such great significance because God, by raising His Son from the dead, wanted to prove to all, that He had completely accepted His substitutionary sacrifice, and is prepared to forgive everyone who in faith draws upon this atoning work, by unreservedly exposing their personal guilt.

Chapter 5

The Consequences of Rejecting the Messiah

Due to the rejection and murder of the Messiah - the eternal God of the OT come in the flesh - by the people of Israel, God turned His back on this people, and gave them up to the brutality, callousness, and evil of other nations. As a result, the fate of this people was calamitous.

The 28th chapter of Deuteronomy is a quite extensive passage in the OT in which is described in minutest detail just what would happen to the people of Israel, should they reject the Messiah.

1. Some Basic Points about the Book of Deuteronomy

This section will be much easier to understand if a few basic points about Deuteronomy are laid out. Deuteronomy is made up of 8 speeches made by Moses in the plains of Moab at the end of the 40-year wandering in the wilderness (16th century BC), shortly before the people of Israel entered the Promised Land (Deuteronomy 1:1-5). In these speeches Moses the lawgiver presented, once more, quite clearly to the people of Israel what God required of them. He depicted how much God would bless them *if they listened to His voice*, and just how God would judge them should they fail to obey His voice.

Deuteronomy can be quite aptly named "The Book of Obedience". The significant words "shama" (= "hear", "obey"), and "shamar" (= "observe", "keep") each appear around 50 times. The word "sachar" (= "remember", "to be mindful of") is also characteristic for this book.

Moses commanded that this book of the Law be very carefully preserved in the Holiest of Holies, beside the Ark of the Covenant, in order for it to stand *as a witness against the people of Israel* (cf. Deuteronomy 31:24-27).

A further characteristic of this book is that it should be read out aloud every seven years to the entire nation of Israel, all the men, women, small children (!), and even foreigners being required to be present (Deuteronomy 31:9-13).

It is very significant that just about in the middle of the book the greatest of all prophets, the Messiah Himself, is spoken of. The prophet Moses spoke to the people of Israel in Deuteronomy 18:17-19:

"And the LORD said unto me, They have well spoken that which they have spoken. I will raise them up a Prophet from among their brethren, like unto thee, and will put my words in his mouth; and he shall speak unto them all that I shall command him. And it shall come to pass, that whosoever will not hearken unto my words[57] which he shall speak in my name, I will require it of him."

Isn't it remarkable that it is precisely in this book of the Bible that the consequences of rejecting the Messiah are spoken about?

In chapter 28 of the book of Deuteronomy God presents the *blessings* and *curses* to the people of Israel through Moses.

Promised Blessings

In the first 14 verses of this chapter, the Eternal One describes through Moses the blessings He wants to bestow upon His people, if they hear His voice:

"(1) And it shall come to pass, if thou shalt hearken diligently unto the voice of the LORD thy God, to observe and to do all his commandments which I command thee this day, that the LORD thy God will set thee on high above all nations of the earth: (2) and all these blessings shall come on thee, and overtake thee, if thou shalt hearken unto the voice of the LORD thy God.

(3) Blessed shalt thou be in the city, and blessed shalt thou be in the field. (4) Blessed shall be the fruit of thy body, and the fruit of thy ground, and the fruit of thy cattle, the increase of thy kine, and the flocks of thy sheep. (5) Blessed shall be thy basket and thy store. (6) Blessed shalt thou be when thou comest in, and blessed shalt thou be when thou goest out.

(7) The LORD shall cause thine enemies that rise up against thee to be smitten before thy face: they shall come out against thee one way, and flee before thee seven ways. (8) The LORD shall command the blessing upon thee in thy storehouses, and in all that thou settest thine hand unto; and he shall bless thee in the land which the LORD thy God giveth thee. (9) The LORD shall establish thee an holy people unto himself, as he hath sworn unto thee, if thou shalt keep the commandments of the LORD thy God, and walk in his ways. (10) And all people of the earth shall see that

thou art called by the name of the LORD; and they shall be afraid of thee.

(11) And the LORD shall make thee plenteous in goods, in the fruit of thy body, and in the fruit of thy cattle, and in the fruit of thy ground, in the land which the LORD sware unto thy fathers to give thee.

(12) The LORD shall open unto thee his good treasure, the heaven to give the rain unto thy land in his season, and to bless all the work of thine hand: and thou shalt lend unto many nations, and thou shalt not borrow.

(13) And the LORD shall make thee the head, and not the tail; and thou shalt be above only, and thou shalt not be beneath; if that thou hearken unto the commandments of the LORD thy God, which I command thee this day, to observe and to do them: (14) and thou shalt not go aside from any of the words which I command thee this day, to the right hand, or to the left, to go after other gods to serve them."

These promised blessings were fulfilled to a very great extent twice in the history of the people of Israel. The first time was during the days of Joshua (16th century BC), as documented in his book: "*And the LORD gave unto Israel all the land which he sware to give unto their fathers; and they possessed it, and dwelt therein. (44) And the LORD gave them rest round about, according to all that he sware unto their fathers: and there stood not a man of all their enemies before them; the LORD delivered all their enemies into their hand. (45) There failed not ought of any good thing which the LORD had spoken unto the house of Israel; all came to pass.*"

The second time this promise became a reality during the time of King Solomon (11th century BC), as confirmed in 1 Kings 8:54-56: *"And it was so, that when Solomon had made an end of praying all this prayer and supplication unto the LORD, he arose from before the altar of the LORD, from kneeling on his knees with his hands spread up to heaven. And he stood, and blessed all the congregation of Israel with a loud voice, saying, Blessed be the LORD, that hath given rest unto his people Israel, according to all that he promised: there hath not failed one word of all his good promise, which he promised by the hand of Moses his servant."*

Curses

In Deuteronomy 28:ff. the Eternal One described to the people of Israel just what curses awaited them should they not remain obedient to His voice. Some of what is detailed in these verses was fulfilled in 722ff. BC, when the Assyrians took the ten tribes of Israel into captivity, and likewise from 606ff. BC, when the remaining two tribes, Judah and Benjamin, were exiled to Babylon.

Here we must qualify the subject. So, with the help of verses 45-68 only, it will be shown in the following how this was fulfilled in the years 70ff. AD as the result of rejecting the Messiah.

Deuteronomy 28:45-68

"(45) Moreover all these curses shall come upon thee, and shall pursue thee, and overtake thee, till thou be destroyed; because thou hearkenedst not unto the voice of the LORD thy God, to keep his commandments and his statutes which he commanded thee: (46) and they shall be upon thee for a sign and for a wonder, and upon thy seed for

ever. (47) Because thou servedst not the LORD thy God with joyfulness, and with gladness of heart, for the abundance of all things; (48) therefore shalt thou serve thine enemies which the LORD shall send against thee, in hunger, and in thirst, and in nakedness, and in want of all things: and he shall put a yoke of iron upon thy neck, until he have destroyed thee.

(49) The LORD shall bring a nation against thee from far, from the end of the earth, as swift as the eagle flieth; a nation whose tongue thou shalt not understand; (50) a nation of fierce countenance, which shall not regard the person of the old, nor shew favour to the young: (51) and he shall eat the fruit of thy cattle, and the fruit of thy land, until thou be destroyed: which also shall not leave thee either corn, wine, or oil, or the increase of thy kine, or flocks of thy sheep, until he have destroyed thee. (52) And he shall besiege thee in all thy gates, until thy high and fenced walls come down, wherein thou trustedst, throughout all thy land: and he shall besiege thee in all thy gates throughout all thy land, which the LORD thy God hath given thee.

(53) And thou shalt eat the fruit of thine own body, the flesh of thy sons and of thy daughters, which the LORD thy God hath given thee, in the siege, and in the straitness, wherewith thine enemies shall distress thee: (54) so that the man that is tender among you, and very delicate, his eye shall be evil toward his brother, and toward the wife of his bosom, and toward the remnant of his children which he shall leave: (55) so that he will not give to any of them of the flesh of his children whom he shall eat: because he hath nothing left him in the siege, and in the straitness, wherewith thine enemies shall distress thee in all thy gates. (56) The tender and delicate woman among you, which would not adventure to set the sole of her foot upon the

ground for delicateness and tenderness, her eye shall be evil toward the husband of her bosom, and toward her son, and toward her daughter, (57) and toward her young one that cometh out from between her feet, and toward her children which she shall bear: for she shall eat them for want of all things secretly in the siege and straitness, wherewith thine enemy shall distress thee in thy gates. (58) If thou wilt not observe to do all the words of this law that are written in this book, that thou mayest fear this glorious and fearful name, THE LORD THY GOD; (59) then the LORD will make thy plagues wonderful, and the plagues of thy seed, even great plagues, and of long continuance, and sore sicknesses, and of long continuance. (60) Moreover he will bring upon thee all the diseases of Egypt, which thou wast afraid of; and they shall cleave unto thee. (61) Also every sickness, and every plague, which is not written in the book of this law, them will the LORD bring upon thee, until thou be destroyed.

(62) And ye shall be left few in number, whereas ye were as the stars of heaven for multitude; because thou wouldest not obey the voice of the LORD thy God.

(63) And it shall come to pass, that as the LORD rejoiced over you to do you good, and to multiply you; so the LORD will rejoice over you to destroy you, and to bring you to nought; and ye shall be plucked from off the land whither thou goest to possess it.

(64) And the LORD shall scatter thee among all people, from the one end of the earth even unto the other; and there thou shalt serve other gods, which neither thou nor thy fathers have known, even wood and stone. (65) And among these nations shalt thou find no ease, neither shall the sole of thy foot have rest: but the LORD shall give thee there a trembling heart, and failing of eyes, and sorrow of mind:

(66) and thy life shall hang in doubt before thee; and thou shalt fear day and night, and shalt have none assurance of thy life: (67) in the morning thou shalt say, Would God it were even! and at even thou shalt say, Would God it were morning! for the fear of thine heart wherewith thou shalt fear, and for the sight of thine eyes which thou shalt see.

(68) And the LORD shall bring thee into Egypt again with ships, by the way whereof I spake unto thee, Thou shalt see it no more again: and there ye shall be sold unto your enemies for bondmen and bondwomen, and no man shall buy you."

The Title for the Fate of the Jews from 70 AD onwards

Verse 45 can be seen as a title for the history of the Jews since the year 70 AD:

"Moreover all these curses shall come upon thee, and shall pursue thee, and overtake thee, till thou be destroyed; because thou hearkenedst not unto the voice of the LORD thy God, to keep his commandments and his statutes which he commanded thee."

The Romans are Coming

Verse 49 depicts a nation from afar that would spring upon the Jews. This was fulfilled by the Romans, who actually came from a long way away and destroyed the State of Israel in the Jewish war (66-73 AD). In the years that followed, they razed the entire country to the ground, especially in the Bar-Kochba revolt (132- 135 AD).

The Eagle of the Legion

The expression that a nation would swoop down upon them "as swift as the eagle flieth" is an interesting one. The historian Flavius Josephus, who was an eye-witness of the events in 70 AD, describes the approach of the Roman army to Jerusalem as follows:

"Now, as Titus was upon his march into the enemy's country, the auxiliaries that were sent by the kings marched first, having all the other auxiliaries with them; after whom followed those that were to prepare the roads, and measure out the camp; then came the commander's baggage, and after that the other soldiers, who were completely armed to support them; then came Titus himself, having with him another select body; and then came the pikemen; after whom came the horse belonging to that legion. All these came before the engines; and after these engines followed the tribunes and the leaders of the cohorts, with their select bodies; after these *came the ensigns, with the eagle*; and before these ensigns, came the trumpeters belonging to them; next these came the main body of the army in their ranks, every rank being six deep."[58]

The Roman Language

It says furthermore that this nation would speak a language that the Jews would not understand. This immediately stands to reason, since the Romans spoke Latin, and not a Semitic language.

A Nation of Fierce Countenance

In Verse 50 it is written that this nation would be "a nation of fierce countenance". Flavius Josephus described this fact in his work "De bello Judaico" ("The Jewish War") VI, 5.1: "While the holy house was on fire, everything was plundered that came to hand, and ten thousand of those that were caught were slain; nor was there commiseration of any age, or any reverence of gravity; but children, and old men, and profane persons, and priests, were all slain in the same manner; so that this war went round all sorts of men, and brought them to destruction, and as well those that made supplication for their lives, as those that defended themselves by fighting."[59]

Famine

Verse 51 talks about how this nation would starve out the Jews, which Flavius Josephus confirms with the following words: "… [the people] were come up from all the country to the feast of unleavened bread, and were on a sudden shut up by an army, which at the very first, occasioned so great a straitness among them, that there came a pestilential destruction upon them, and soon afterward such a famine as destroyed them more suddenly."[60]

The Entire Country Under Siege; the Jewish Fortifications

In verse 52 it is said that the siege of this nation would occur in every gate throughout the whole land, and that the high and strong walls, which the Jews would put their trust in, would fall throughout the land.

Flavius Josephus depicts in detail the destruction of the walls of Jerusalem, after first describing the imposing walls of that city in Book V of "The Jewish War".

In Book VI, 9.4 he writes: "… the Romans set fire to the extreme parts of the city, and burnt them down, and entirely demolished its walls".[61]

In Verse 52 it tells us that all the fortifications throughout the entire land would be destroyed. Rome conquered not only Jerusalem, but the entire land of Israel. The first conquests started in 66 AD, and the final resistance of the Jews was shattered by the Romans in 73 AD, when the fortress of Masada, in the Judean desert near the Dead Sea, fell into the hands of the Romans.

Furthermore the following is worth mentioning in this regard: The historian Dio Cassius (2nd/3rd Century AD) reports that, subsequent to the Bar-Kochba revolt, the Romans destroyed 50 fortresses and 985 towns.[62]

Cannibalism

In verses 53-57 there is mention of cannibalism which would come about as a result of the Roman siege. Flavius Josephus confirmed this in his "History of the Jewish War" VI, 3.4.

Plagues

In Verse 59 plagues, amongst other things, is spoken about. The "History of The Jewish Wars" VI, 9.3 confirms that during the siege of Jerusalem plagues broke out.

Few in Number

Verse 62 says that the Jews would only survive to be few in number, instead of being a huge population. Flavius Josephus reports: "Now the number of those that were carried captive during this whole war was collected to be ninety-seven thousand; as was the number of those that perished during the whole siege, eleven hundred thousand."[63]

Scattered throughout the World

In verses 63 and 64 it is shown that the Jews would be uprooted from their country and scattered among all the other peoples, in fact "from one end of the earth to the other". This is a well known fact, that the Jews were scattered literally throughout the entire world in the wake of 70 AD.[64]

The fulfilment of verse 68 is also confirmed in by history. Countless survivors of the Jewish War were shipped off and transported to the slave markets in Egypt. However, supply soon exceeded demand, so the slaves became worthless.[65]

No Rest and Permanent Fear

In verses 65-67 it is emphasized that the Jews would never have rest among those nations, and would always be living in fear for their lives. The history of the Jews from then on is enough proof of this fact. In the book, "The Facts about The Jews," it describes the history of the Jews since 70 AD from a Jewish perspective in the following characteristic fashion: "Insecurity was the main feature of Jewish experience in countless foreign lands".[66]

The Fulfilment of Deuteronomy 28:65-67

Here is a summary of some of the main events comprising the fulfilment of Deuteronomy 28:65-67:[67]

- 70 AD: The Jewish war, with more than 1,000,000 dead.
- 115-117 AD: The Jewish expulsion from Cyprus, revolts against the Romans in various places: hundreds of thousands dead.
- 132-135 AD: The revolt led by Bar-Kochba, as a result of which 530,000 Jews perished under the Emperor Hadrian, and as many again dying in the aftermath of the war (of famine and disease).
- 415 AD: 100,000 Jews looted and driven out of Alexandria.
- 499 AD: Savage persecution of the Jews in Persia.
- 581 AD: Persecution in Babylon and Persia.
- 632 AD: Expulsion from Arabia by the Muslims.
- 640, 721, 873, and 930 AD: Suppression of the Jews in the Byzantine Empire.
- 1015 AD: 12,000 Jews murdered in Cairo.
- 1033 AD: 6,000 Jews murdered in Fez (Morocco).
- 1066 AD: over 5,000 Jews murdered in Granada.
- 1096 AD: 12,000 Jews murdered in the Rhine valley.
- 1099 AD: Massacre of Jews in Jerusalem.
- 1146 AD: Suppression of the Jews in Spain.
- 1150 AD: Extensive persecution of the Jews in Tunisia.
- 1232 AD: Massacre of the Jews in Marrakesh and persecution of Jews throughout Morocco.
- 1236 AD: 3,000 Jews killed in France.
- 1270 AD: Mass persecution of Jews in Tunisia.
- 1290 AD: Jews expelled from England (c. 370,000).

- 1298 AD: 100,000 Jews murdered in Franconia and in Bavaria.
- 1306 AD: Expulsion of the Jews from France.
- 1348/49 AD: The Black Death: 1,000,000 Jews massacred in Europe.
- 1355 AD: A mob of Arabs massacre 12,000 Jews in Toledo (Spain).
- 1345-1360 AD: Expulsion of Jews from Hungary.
- 1391 AD: Suppression of the Jews in Spain, with 50,000 murdered in Palma.
- 1420 AD: Eradication of the entire Jewish community in Toulouse (France).
- 1421 AD: Expulsion of the Jews from Austria.
- 1492 AD: 160,000 Jews expelled from Spain.
- 1495 AD: The Jews expelled from Lithuania.
- 1497 AD: The Jews expelled from Sicily and Sardinia; expulsion from Portugal.
- 1502 AD: The Jews of Rhodes suppressed, expelled and enslaved.
- 1541 AD: Expulsion of the Jews from the Kingdom of Naples.
- 1648-1656 AD: 100,000 Jews murdered in the Chmielnicki massacre in Poland.
- 1727 and 1747 AD: Expulsions from Russia.
- 1785 AD: Savage persecution of the Jews in Libya.
- 1864-1880 AD: More than 500 Jews murdered in Morocco.
- 1871-1921 AD: Terrible and savage persecution of the Jews in many cities of Russia.
- 1939-1945 AD: 6,000,000 Jews murdered by the German Nazis and their European collaborators.

A shocking total: In the time from 70 AD to the present day over 13,000,000 Jews have lost their lives due to war and persecution.

Other prophets also foretold the fate of the Jews after the year 70 AD. In Jeremiah 29:18-19, for example, it says:

"And I will persecute them with the sword, with the famine, and with the pestilence, and will deliver them to be removed to all the kingdoms of the earth, to be a curse, and an astonishment, and an hissing, and a reproach, among all the nations whither I have driven them: because they have not hearkened to my words,[68] saith the LORD."

In Jeremiah 30:12-15 the reason for the fate of the Jews is mentioned again. Likewise the prophets Isaiah, Ezekiel, Daniel, Hosea, Micah, and Zechariah, amongst others, give prophetic insights into this period of Jewish history.

2. The Land of Israel will become a Desert

Regarding the Land of Israel, which "flowed with milk and honey," and would be irrigated by two rainy seasons, God said :

"And I will scatter you among the heathen, and will draw out a sword after you: and your land shall be desolate, and your cities waste. Then shall the land enjoy her sabbaths, as long as it lieth desolate, and ye be in your enemies' land; even then shall the land rest, and enjoy her sabbaths. As long as it lieth desolate it shall rest; because it did not rest in your sabbaths, when ye dwelt upon it" (Leviticus 26:33-35).

"... I scattered them with a whirlwind among all the

nations whom they knew not. Thus the land was desolate after them, that no man passed through nor returned: for they laid the pleasant land desolate" (Zechariah 7:14).

Similar prophecies are to be found in further passages (cf. Deuteronomy 11:16-17 [rain!]; Isaiah 6:11-12; 5:6; Jeremiah 3:2-3).

History gives us enough evidence as to how this was all fulfilled literally. In both of the Jewish revolts (66-73 AD and 132-135 AD) the Romans laid waste the Land of Israel to quite an unimaginable extent.[69] The armies of the Islamic people conquered the entire Holy Land between 636 AD and 640 AD. The non-Muslim population was subjected to a heavy and humiliating "Jizya (protection) tax", resulting in the rapid depopulation of the land. Because the Arabs weren't inclined to work the fields, leaving their cattle to graze on what grew of its own accord, and since the Turks hardly replanted a tree where they had felled one, and even levelled tree taxes which were so exorbitantly high in the last century so that people preferred to fell trees rather than pay the tax, in the course of time the Land of the Bible increasingly deteriorated into a desert area.[70] The most fruitful areas, being the valley of Jezreel, the Jordan valley, and the coastline (from Acco up to Jaffa), turned into malaria-infested marshland. The wooded mountains of the Land of Israel were felled absurdly, the roads just crumbled to pieces, and the desert possessed the whole Land for itself.[71]

Mark Twain visited the Land of the Bible in 1867. His report registered concern: "Of all the lands there are for dismal scenery, I think Palestine must be the prince. The hills are barren, they are dull of color, they are unpicturesque in shape. The valleys are unsightly deserts fringed with a feeble vegetation that has an expression about it of being sorrowful and despondent. The Dead Sea and the Sea of Galilee sleep in the midst of a vast stretch of hill and plain wherein the eye rests upon no pleasant tint, no striking object, no soft picture dreaming in a purple haze or mottled with the shadows of the clouds. Every outline is harsh, every feature is distinct, there is no perspective -- distance works no enchantment here. It is a hopeless, dreary, heart-broken land. ".[72]

It should have now become clear that the Jewish people, although they knew from the OT since the wilderness wanderings (1606-1566 BC) what would happen to them should they not listen to the voice of the Eternal One and thus also reject the Messiah, has experienced the total truth of Deuteronomy 28 and all the other passages in the OT.

God gave the Jewish people over to the barbarism, brutality and evil of the other nations many times. All of these nations which did these things *by their own will and on their own authority* (they were not predetermined, but simply *foreknown*) God will yet bring into an unimaginably great and fearful judgement (cf. e.g. Jeremiah 30:11; Joel 3:1-4)!

3. Israel – A Model and Warning for All People

The following question bears thinking over: Are non-Jews better than Jews, and wouldn't another people have hated and murdered the Messiah?

It must be quite clear to us by now that other peoples are not a jot better, and would have done exactly the same!

This being the case, what is the difference between non-Jews and Jews?

It is quite simple: The Eternal One chose the Israelites as His own people out of all nations (cf. Deuteronomy 7), to be a "prototype", an "example" for all other nations. Through Israel God wanted to demonstrate to all other people, what would happen if they took Him at His word, and what would happen if they didn't obey His word.

Moses wrote in Deuteronomy 28:46 judgements and punishments would hang over the Jews as "signs and wonders" (Hebrew "le'oth ulemopheth"). This expression can literally be rendered as *"warning and example"*.[73] For whom then should the terrible fate of the Jews be a warning and an example?

God didn't just send the Messiah for the Jews alone, but *for all the people*. Through the prophet Isaiah He said of the Messiah:

"It is a light thing that thou shouldest be my servant to raise up the tribes of Jacob, and to restore the preserved of Israel: I will also give thee for a light to the Gentiles, that thou mayest be my salvation unto the end of the earth" (Isaiah 49:6).

God is offering the Messiah as the Redeemer to *all people*! This prompts the question for us, whether we (i.e. every individual) are prepared to accept the Lord Jesus as our Saviour or not. Just like Israel, each one of us has to make a decision! God sets His *blessing* or His *curse* before each inhabitant of the Earth. However, the blessings and curses *for the example Israel* were tem-

porary, but *the* blessings and *the* curses set before the world are eternal.

Blessing	**Curse**
The Father's house John 14:2	*The gnawing worm* Mark 9:48
The marriage of the Lamb Revelation 19:7	*Eternal punishment* Matthew 25:46
Eternal joy Isaiah 51:11	*Unquenchable fire* Mark 9:48
Eternal salvation Hebrews 5:9	*Eternal judgement* Hebrews 6:2
Eternal comfort 2 Thessalonians 2:16	*Eternal destruction* 2 Thessalonians 1:9
Rest for God's people Hebrews 4:9	*Condemnation of unbelievers* Mark 16:16
Eternal inheritance Hebrews 9:15	*The portion of the devil and the portion of all those*
God's presence Revelation 21:3	*whose names are not in the Lamb's book of life* Revelation 20:15
Eternal glory 2 Timothy 2:10	*Outer darkness* Matthew 22:13

Seeing God's face	*Eternal weeping*
Revelation 22:4	Matthew 13:42
Eternal life	*The second death*
John 17:2-3	Revelation 20:14
Eternal worship of God	*Eternal abhorrence and shame*
Revelation 7:11-12	Daniel 11:2

"See, I have set before thee this day life and good, and death and evil; ... therefore choose life, that both thou and thy seed may live" (Deuteronomy 30:15,19).[74]

Chapter 6

Looking Ahead to the Messiah's Second Coming

1. The Restoration of the Land of Israel

Has God disowned and abandoned His people forever? The answer is, of course, a resounding, No! (cf. Romans 11:1).

Just as the prophets said that, after the rejection of the Messiah, the Jews would be scattered over the whole world, they also prophesied that God would gather them all together and make them into a state.

The Land of Palestine was liberated for the Jewish people by the First World War (1914-1918). The Second World War with its dreadful persecution of the Jews and concentration camps awakened the profound desires of hundreds of thousands of Jews hearts' to be able to return to their own Land of Israel - indeed, to such an extent as never before.

The prophet Jeremiah spoke of the "fishermen and hunters" which God would put use in order to bring back the Jews to their Land from all the countries in which He had scattered them:

"Therefore, behold, the days come, saith the Lord, that it shall no more be said, The Lord liveth, that brought up

the children of Israel out of the land of Egypt; but, The Lord liveth, that brought up the children of Israel from the land of the north, and from all the lands whither he had driven them: and I will bring them again into their land that I gave unto their fathers. Behold, I will send for many fishers, saith the Lord, and they shall fish them; and after will I send for many hunters, and they shall hunt them from every mountain, and from every hill, and out of the holes of the rocks" (Jeremiah 16:14-16).

Doesn't the term "fishermen" bring the Zionists to mind who, with strenuous effort, since 1897 wanted to "fish" for Jews to return to the Land of Israel? And don't the "hunters", who would go into action after(!) the fishermen, remind us of Hitler and his satellites who hunted down the Jews in droves to their homeland?

In 1948, on the night of the 14th to the 15th May, 400 Zionists sat down together, and David Ben Gurion, rising, delivered an astounding message as a new president to the world: "I, as Ben Gurion, am addressing the country of Israel as the new Prime Minister. Here is the State of Israel. 2,000 years have passed. When the time for God has come, no one can withstand Him!"[75]

The prophecies have been literally fulfilled even here. Here are a few examples:

"Therefore say, Thus saith the Lord God; I will even gather you from the people, and assemble you out of the countries where ye have been scattered, and I will give you the land of Israel" (Ezekiel 11:17).

"And say unto them, Thus saith the Lord God; Behold, I will take the children of Israel from among the heathen, whither they be gone, and will gather them on every side, and bring them into their own land" (Ezekiel 37:21).

"For I will take you from among the heathen, and gather you out of all countries, and will bring you into your own land" (Ezekiel 36:24).

But what would become of the Land of Israel that beforehand was a desert?

There are plenty of Bible passages which shed light on this question, a good example being Psalm 107. In this chapter of the Bible the whole history of the people of Israel from the Exodus from Egypt, up to the time when the Messiah will come for the second time is described.[76] Verses 33-34 are still speaking about events since the year 70 AD, but verses 35-38 describe the period after 1948. It says:

"He [the Eternal One] turneth the wilderness into a standing water, and dry ground into watersprings. And there he maketh the hungry to dwell, that they [i.e. the Jews] may prepare a city for habitation; and sow the fields, and plant vineyards, which may yield fruits of increase. He blesseth them also, so that they are multiplied greatly; and suffereth not their cattle to decrease."

Here, the desert is to blossom again! In actual fact the Land of Israel has once again become a land of which it can be said it "overflows with milk and honey". Building on the ground has been well organised. The yields from grain, vegetable, citrus, wine, and olive plantations have grown steadily over decades. Since the Jews have populated the land of their forefathers, the climate has changed in the most incredible way, so that the two rainy seasons can once again be counted on.

2. The Connection between the Restoration of Israel and the Messiah's Second Coming

What has this all to do with the Messiah's Second Coming? Many passages in the OT describe the "suffering Messiah" who would be rejected. *The result of this occurrence would be the scattering of the Jewish people throughout the entire world.*[77]

On the other hand, however, there are a whole series of passages in the OT which talk of the "triumphant Messiah", and declare that, *shortly before His appearance, the Jews in part would return from worldwide dispersion.*

This is clear from Ezekiel 37, for example. Verses 12-14 talk about the return of the Jews from the worldwide dispersion, and then in verses 24-28 the "triumphing Messiah" and His glorious reign is spoken of. There He is called "my servant David" (David = the Beloved; cf. Ephesians 1:6). This is a well-known term for the Messiah in Judaism.

How will the Jews[78] react to the returning Messiah? Chapters 12 and 13 of Zechariah provides information in answer to this question. In chapter 12:10-12 it says:

"I will pour upon the house of David, and upon the inhabitants of Jerusalem, the spirit of grace and of supplications: and they shall look upon me whom they have pierced, and they shall mourn for him, as one mourneth for his only son, and shall be in bitterness for him, as one that is in bitterness for his firstborn. In that day shall there be a great mourning in Jerusalem, as the mourning of Hadadrimmon in the valley of Megiddon.79 And the land shall mourn."

This passage is interpreted as Messianic in the Babylonian Talmud, Sukkah 52a!

We have now seen just how Biblical prophecy has been fulfilled literally in the past and even up to our own time, and, regarding the future, is likewise about to be fulfilled.

Epilogue

It is clear that an exhaustive study of Messianic prophecy cannot be conducted within the confines of the comments at hand. I trust, however, that I have provided convincing evidence that

1. Jesus of Nazareth is indeed the prophesied Messiah of the OT, and
2. the wellbeing and wretchedness of each individual person depends on the acceptance or rejection of the Lord Jesus as the Messiah and Redeemer.

Appendix

Endnotes

1   For an account of the chronological information in the OT cf. Roger Liebi: Zur Chronologie des OT, Skript, 2006 (free from info@rogerliebi.ch).

2   The Biblical manuscripts from Qumran have been published in English translation in one volume: ABEGG, M./FLINT, P./ ULRICH, E.: The Dead Sea Scrolls Bible, The oldest known Bible translated for the first time into English, San Francisco 1999.

3   ABEGG, M./FLINT, P./ULRICH, E.: The Dead Sea Scrolls Bible, The oldest known Bible translated for the first time into English, loc. cit., p.267.

4   LAMORTE, A.: Israel – sein Land und sein Buch, Beatenberg 1970, p.28; mistakes in translation of the German version corrected according to: LAMORTE, A.: Les découvertes archéologiques de la mer morte – fantaisie ou histoire?, Bevaix, p.34.

5   TREVER, J.C.: Scrolls From Qumran Cave I (The Great Isaiah Scroll), Jerusalem 1972.

6   CROSS, F.M.: The Ancient Library of Qumrân, and Modern Biblical Studies, London 1958, p. 120.

7   CROSS, F.M., loc. cit., p.122.

8   ABEGG, M./FLINT, P./ULRICH, E.: The Dead Sea Scrolls Bible, The oldest known Bible translated for the first time into English, loc. cit., p.482.

9   The Latin word "Septuaginta" means "seventy".

10 The Septuagint Greek and English, Bagster and Sons Ltd., London, Introduction, p. 1.

11 The Septuagint Greek and English, loc. cit., p. 1. Cf. John 10:34 with Psalm 82:6 and 1 Corinthians 14:21 with Isaiah 28:11-12.

12 King James Translation of the Bible (with Apocrypha), The Prologue of the Wisdom of Jesus the Son of Sirach.

13 Standard edition of the Septuagint; SEPTUAGINTA, ed. Alfred Rahlfs, Stuttgart 1935.

14 Recommended editions:

15 JOSEPHUS: The Jewish War, translated by H. St. J. Thackeray, 3 volumes, Loeb Classical Library, Cambridge, Massachusetts/ London 2004.

16 JOSEPHUS: Wars of the Jews, in: Whiston, W.: The Complete Works of Josephus, Grand Rapids 1981, pp. 427-605..

17 A good English edition: JOSEPHUS: Antiquities of the Jews, in:

Whiston, W.: The Complete Works of Josephus, Grand Rapids 1981, pp. 23-426.

18   Editions of the Talmud:

19   Complete English translation:

20   Hebrew-Aramaic Original Text: THALMUD BAVLI, 11 volumes, Yerushalayim, no date (standard edition used generally in Orthodox Judaism).

21   Hebrew-Aramaic edition with English translation: THE SONCINO TALMUD, Classic Judaic Library, CD-ROM, Version Iic3, Judaic Press, Inc., Brooklyn, New York.

22   Hebrew-Aramaic edition in: BAR ILAN'S JUDAIC LIBRARY, Bar Ilan University, Responsa Project, CD-ROM, Version 5.

23   ALAND, K.: Kurz gefasste Liste der griechischen Handschriften des NT (1. Gesamtübersicht), Berlin 1963; ALAND, K and B.: The Text of the New Testament: an introduction to the critical editions and to the theory and practice of modern textual criticism, (translated by E.F. Rhodes), Grand Rapids: Eerdmans, c. 1987, loc. cit., p. 77.

24   PACHE, R.: Inspiration und Autorität der Bibel, Wuppertal, 2. Auflage 1976, p. 187.

25   ALAND, K and B.: The Text of the New Testament: an introduction to the critical editions and to the theory and practice of modern textual criticism, (translated by E.F. Rhodes), Grand Rapids: Eerdmans, c. 1987, loc. cit., pp. 83ff. COMFORT, PH.W.: Early Manuscripts & Modern Transcriptions of the New Testament, Grand Rapids 1990. LIEBI, R.: Paulusbriefe neu bestätigt, factum 11/12-1989, p. 458.

26   MAUERHOFER, E.: Einleitung in die Schriften des Neuen Testaments, vol. 1, Neuhausen/Stuttgart 1995, pp. 39-250.

27   Cf. also: GITT, W.: Prophetie – Gottes Offenbarung in Raum und Zeit, factum 1 / 2-1981.

28   GESENIUS, W./KAUTZSCH, E.: Gesenius' Hebrew Grammar, 2nd English edition edited by A.E. Cowley, Oxford 1910, pp. 312-313: Explanation of the use of the Hebrew perfect: "To express *future* actions, when the speaker intends by an express assurance to represent them as finished, or as equivalent to accomplished facts: … This use of the perfect occurs most frequently in prophetic language (*perfectum propheticum*). The prophet so transports himself in imagination into the future that he describes the future event as if it had been already seen or heard by him …"

29   Cf. ANDERSON, R.: The Coming prince, 10th edition, Grand Rapids 1957, p. 67-75.

30 Quoted in BRUCE, F.F.: Jesus and Christian Origins outside the New Testament, London 1984, p. 12. Complete edition of the Histories by Tacitus: TACITUS, P.C.: Histories, Latin-English, translated by C.H. Moore, Cambridge, Massachusetts/London 1989.

31 Quoted in: BRUCE, F.F.: Jesus and Christian Origins outside the New Testament, loc. cit., p. 26.

32 Quoted in BRUCE, F.F.: The New Testament Documents: Are They Reliable?, Fifth revised edition, Downers Grove 1942, p. 119.

33 Rashi's commentaries can be found in: miqra'oth gedololoth, volumes I-VIII, Jerusalem 1972.

34 E.g. Babylonian Talmud, Nazir 32b; JOSEPHUS: Antiquities of the Jews, X, 11.7; JOSEPHUS: The Jewish War, IV, 6.3 and VI, 5.4.

35 Quoted in MEISTER, A: Die Erfüllung der messianischen Verheißung des AT durch Jesus von Nazareth, Prof. S. Külling (ed.), Bettingen, no date, p. 19. English translation by Boaz Cohen (accessed on 17/1/14): http://en.wikisource.org/wiki/Epistle_to_Yemen/Complete.

36 Babylonian Talmud, Sanhedrin 98b.

37 EDERSHEIM, A.: The Life and Times of Jesus the Messiah, Reprinted Edition, Grand Rapids 1986, p. 712-713. On pp. 710-741 this work contains a comprehensive summary of passages in rabbinic literature in which Old Testament statements are interpreted as Messianic.

38 "Targumim" (plural of "Targum") are Aramaic paraphrases and translations of almost the whole of the OT. Following the Babylonian captivity Aramaic increasingly replaced Hebrew as the national language. From this time on, therefore, when the OT was read aloud in the synagogue the text was always translated into Aramaic. At first this occurred orally and off by heart. Later these translation traditions were fixed in writing in the Targumim. Since they contain explanatory supplements, they provide information about theological thought in Judaism even well back into the pre-Christian era.

39 To the most ancient and most important Targumim belong the Targum Onkelos on the five books of Moses (origins: c. 2nd century AD; later there was more re-editing) and the Targum Jonathan Ben Uzziel on the prophets (origin: c. 1st-2nd century AD; re-editing: 3rd-5th century AD?).

40 Edition with Targumim: miqra'oth gedololoth, volumes I-VIII, loc. cit.

41 Edition in: BAR ILAN'S JUDAIC LIBRARY, loc. cit.

42 In connection with the people of Israel the "shevet" is also an

expression of the fact that the tribe possessing it from God is viewed as the responsible witness to the other nations.

43 It must be proved that Matthew 1 actually gives an account of Joseph's genealogy and Luke 3 that of Mary's: In Matthew 1:16 it says: "And Jacob *begat* Joseph the husband of Mary." It follows from this that Jacob was Joseph's actual father. In Luke 3:23, however, it says in the King James Version; "… Joseph, which was the son of Heli …" But the word "son" is not given in the Greek! He was the son of Jacob and only the son-in-law of Heli, Mary's father.

44 Edition with Targum Onkelos: miqra'oth gedololoth, volumes I-VIII, loc. cit.

45 For Ramsay cf.: BRUCE, F.F.: The New Testament Documents: Are They Reliable?, loc. cit., p. 92. For modern research which confirm the reliability of Luke's account cf. the following standard work: HEMER, C.J.: the Book of Acts in the Setting of Hellenistic History, Tübingen 1989.

46 Edition in: miqra'oth gedololoth, volumes I-VIII, loc. cit.

47 On the cruelty of King Archelaus cf. JOSEPHUS: "The Jewish War", II, 7.3.

48 Cf. JOSEPHUS: "The Jewish War", I, 33.

49 The punctuation of the Hebrew text which forms the basis of this quote is supported by the Septuagint translation of Isaiah 40:3 (cf. also Matthew 3:3). According to other punctuation this passage can be translated in the following way (cf. the Complete Jewish Bible translation by David Stern): "A voice of one crying: In the desert prepare the way of the LORD."

50 Cf. e.g. His prophecies concerning the destruction of Jerusalem (Luke 19:41-44 and 21:20-24). His prophecy in Luke 21:20-14 led to the rescue of all Jewish Christians before the catastrophe in 70 AD. In 68 AD the Roman legions conquered the area of Judea bit by bit and continued to encircle the centre, Jerusalem. The Roman Empire fell into confusion, prompted by the suicide of the emperor Nero, which caused the war against the Jews to falter. So the Jewish Christians, loyal to the word of their Lord, could leave Jerusalem and find security in Pella on the other side of the Jordan. Only in 70 AD was the siege wall around Jerusalem finally sealed, sealing the terrible fate of the city (cf. EUSEBIUS: Church History from A.D. 1-324, Translated with Prolegomena and Notes by Arthur Cushman McGiffert, in: THE MASTER CHRISTIAN LIBRARY, loc. cit., The Nicene and Post-Nicene Fathers, Second Series, Volume I, by Philip Schaff, III,5.).

51   For the Messianic interpretation of Psalm 69 in the NT cf. Romans 15:3.

52   Cf. e.g. WILSON, W.: New Wilson's Old Testament Word Studies, Grand Rapids 1978, p. 265.

53   Pesiqta Rabbati, Pisqua 36:161b on Isaiah 60:1-2 and Pisqua 37:162b on Isaiah 60:10. A French translation of this passage can be found in: BRIERRE-NARBONNE, J-J.: Les prophéties messianiques de l'Ancien Testament dans la littérature juive en accord avec le Nouveau Testament, avec une introduction sur la littérature messianique juive apocryphe, targoumique, midrachique, zoharique et rabbinique, Paris 1933, p. 18-19.

54   The OT clearly distinguishes between clean and unclean animals (cf. Leviticus 11; Deuteronomy 14). According to this distinction the dog falls into the category of unclean animals. Therefore, the non-Israelites who did not belong to the people of God (= Israel) were referred to vividly with the expression "dogs" (cf. Acts 10-11). It is in no way being used here as an insult!

55   The translation "pierced" is absolutely correct. The LXX also understands the Hebrew expression in this way. "ka'ari" stands for "ka'arim" and must, therefore, be understood as the Kal participle active plural masculine of the root "kur". Cf. DAVIDSON, B.: The Analytical Hebrew and Chaldee Lexicon, London 1970, p. 45 (XXI,1,1) and p. 367.

56   Quoted in: GREEN, M.: You Can't Be Serious. 12 Popular Reasons For Avoiding Jesus, Monarch Books 2005, p. 92. This quote is also found in: JACOBI, F.: Die Fragmente der griechischen Historiker II B, Berlin 1929, p. 1157.

57   Cf. the footnote in the Elberfelder Translation for Isaiah 53:9.

58   Breaking the legs would lead more quickly to death.

59   The text in French translation in: NARBONNE, J-J.: Les prophéties messianiques de l'Ancien Testament dans la literature juive en accord avec le Nouveau Testament, loc. cit., p. 45.

60   Text in: BAR ILAN'S JUDAIC LIBRARY, loc. cit.

61   Text in: BAR ILAN'S JUDAIC LIBRARY, loc. cit.

62   Quoted in MEISTER, A.: Die Erfüllung der messianischen Verheißung des AT durch Jesus von Nazareth, loc. Cit., p. 13.

63   Quoted in MEISTER, A.: Die Erfüllung der messianischen Verheißung des AT durch Jesus von Nazareth, loc. cit., p. 13.

64   In this translation almost all suffering is rendered this way by linguistic acts of violence. This is obviously the result of later re-editing from polemical motives.

65   Cf. the quote from Jeremiah (29:18) under "The Fulfilment of

Deuteronomy 28:65-67" in this chapter.

66 Quoted in JOSPEHUS: The Jewish War, V, 2.1, in: Whiston, loc. cit. (italics by the author).

67 Quoted in JOSPEHUS: The Jewish War, loc. cit., VI, 5.1.

68 Quoted in JOSPEHUS: The Jewish War, loc. cit., VI, 9.3.

69 Quoted in JOSPEHUS: The Jewish War, loc. cit., VI, 9.4.

70 DIO, C.: Historia Romana LXIX,14,3.

71 Quoted in JOSPEHUS: The Jewish War, loc. cit., VI, 9.3.

72 Cf., for example, Neues Lexicon, Zürich 1965, "Juden", p. 1925.

73 Cf. JOSPEHUS: The Jewish War, loc. cit., VI, 9.2 and the Stuttgarter Jubiläumsbibel 1949, footnote to Deuteronomy 28:68.

74 From: Facts About Israel, Informationsabteilung beim Außenministerium, Jerusalem 1974, p. 32.

75 From: Facts About Israel, Israel Ministry of Foreign Affairs, Jerusalem 2010, p. 18-34 and AEBI, E.: Geheimnis Israel, Zürich 1961; ELLENBERGER, H.: Die Leiden und Verfolgungen der Juden und ihre Beschützer in chronologischer Reihenfolge, 2. Auflage, Prag 1882; SULGER BÜEL, E.: Der schwarze Tod, „ethos" 3/91, pp. 48-51.

76 Cf. the quote from Deuteronomy 18:17-19 under "1. Some Basic Points in the Book of Deuteronomy" in this chapter.

77 Cf. ROTH, C.: Geschichte der Juden, 2. Ergänzte Auflage, Teissen 1964, pp. 66-70 and 132-135.

78 Cf. PACHE, R.: Die Wiederkunft Christi, 5. Auflage, Wuppertal 1968, p. 245. The Return of Jesus Christ, Moody Press 1955.

79 NEGEV, A.: Funde und Schätze im Land der Bibel, Stuttgart 1978, p. 36-37.

80 TWAIN, M.: Innocents Abroad, Chapter LVI, 1869.

81 Cf. DAVIDSON, B.: The Analytical Hebrew and Chaldee Lexicon, loc. cit. and footnote in the Elberfelder Translation for Isaiah 8:18.

82 This summary is, to a great extent, taken from the tract "Welches ist Ihr Endziel?" by KIENE, P.F., Beröa-Verlag, with kind permission from the author.

83 Quoted in AEBI, E.; Geheimnis Israel, loc. cit., p. 23.

84 Cf. OUWENEEL, W.J.: Die Zukunft der Stadt des großen Königs, 2. Auflage, Neustadt/Weinstraße 1978, on Psalm 107 (page numbers according to the index of Scripture passages in the appendix).

85 Cf. also Isaiah 8:13-15; Psalm 69:22ff., for example, alongside the passages already quoted (the previous verses describe the Messiah's suffering).

86   The "believing remnant" of the Jews is intended here; cf. Isaiah
      10:20-22; 28:5; 37:31-32; Zephaniah 2:7 and Zechariah 8:6,11.
87   Cf. 2 Chronicles 35:22ff.

Bible Passages

Quotations of Bible passages are taken from the King James Version
(otherwise known as the Authorized Version).

Original Language Editions of the OT and NT

- Biblia Hebraica Stuttgartensia, Thora, Neviim Ukhtuvim,
  4th edition, Stuttgart 1990.
- Novum Testamentum Graece, nestle-Aland, 27th edition,
  Stuttgart 1993.
- The Greek New Testament, United Bible Societies, Fourth
  Revised Edition, 1993.
- ROBINSON, M.A./PIERPONT, W.G.: The New Testament
  in the Original Greek: Byzantine Textform, arranged and
  compiled by Maurice A. Robinson and William G. Pier-
  pont, Southborough 2005.

Roger Liebi's Bibliography

- The Messiah in the Temple. The Symbolism of the Second Temple
  in Light of the New Testament, CMV Hagedorn, Düsseldorf, 2012.
  Der Messias im Tempel. Die Symbolik des Zweiten Tempels im
  Licht des Neuen Testaments, 2. Auflage, Bielefeld 2007 (Erstauflage
  2002; online: clv.de). Translation: French.
- Are We Really Living in the End Times?
- Der Verheissene Erlöser, ihre Erfüllung und ihre historische Echtheit, 7. Auflage, Bielefeld 2007 (online: clv.de). Entspricht dem
  früheren Titel: Erfüllte Prophetie, Messianische Prophetie - ihre
  Erfüllung und historische Echtheit, 5. Auflage, Berneck 1990 (Erstauflage 1983). Translations: French, Dutch, Italian, Hungarian
  and Tajik (English edition in progress).

- Weltgeschichte im Visier des Propheten Daniel, 8. Auflage, Bielefeld 2009 (Erstauflage 1986). Translations: French, Spanish, Polish, Russian, Slovak, Bulgarian and Hungarian (online: clv.de). (English edition in progress.)
- Rockmusik! Daten, Fakten, Hintergründe, Ausdruck einer Jugend in einem sterbenden Zeitalter, 4. Auflage, Zürich 1995 (Erstauflage 1987).
- Introduction à la poésie hébraïque, in: Cahiers des REBS. No. 8, 1994 (= Übersetzung eines factum-Artikels von Mai 1988).
- Einführung in die vier Evangelien, Zürich 1990. Translations: Italian and Hungarian.
- Der Mensch - ein sprechender Affe? Sprachwissenschaft contra Bibel, Berneck 1991.
- New Age! Kritische Bemerkungen zum gegenwärtigen Esoterik-Boom, Zürich 1991. Translations: French, Hungarian, Russian, Slovak, Spanish (English edition in progress).
- Wolfgang Amadeus Mozart, Zwischen Ideal und Abgrund, Berneck 1991.
- Défendre la foi chrétienne, in: Cahiers des REBS. No. 14, 1995 (Seminar 1991).
- Israel und das Schicksal des Irak, Unruheherd Nahost im Licht der Bibel, 5. Auflage, Berneck 2003 (Erstauflage 1993). Translations: Italian, Spanish and Hungarian.
- Das neue Europa - Hoffnung oder Illusion? 6. Auflage, Berneck 2004 (Erstauflage 1994).
- Ist die Bibel glaubwürdig? Die Bibel ihre Autorität und Zuverlässigkeit, Zürich 1995. Translation: Hungarian.
- Jerusalem - Hindernis für den Weltfrieden, Das Drama des jüdischen Tempels, 5. Auflage, Berneck 2003 (Erstauflage 1994). Translations: French, Dutch and Hungarian.
- La Palabra de Verdad – Unidad y Diversidad de la Biblia, Porto Alegre 2003.
- Hesekiel, Ezra Studienreihe, Pfäffikon / Düsseldorf 2001 (Koautor: Joël Prohin). Entspricht weitgehend dem französischen Original: Le prophète Ezéchiel, in: Sondez les Ecritures, Bd. 9, Koautor: Joël Prohin, Valence 1995.
- Livre des Proverbes, in: Sondez les Ecritures. Bd. 5, Koautor: Joël Prohin, Valence 1995.
- So entstand das Christentum: Die Welt der Evangelien und der Apostelgeschichte völlig neu erlebt. In: R. Liebi, D. Hunt, A. A. Seibel, N. Lieth: Prophetie – zeitnah – zeitwahr – zeitklar. Pfäffikon 2000, S. 9–39. Translation: Portugese.

- Ein neuer Blick auf die Passionswoche und ihren jüdischen Hintergrund, Das Schönste kommt noch – die himmlische Herrlichkeit im Buch der Offenbarung, in: L. Gassmann, N. Lieth, R. Liebi: Was uns die Zukunft bringt, Pfäffikon, 2002, p. 8–75.
- Herkunft und Entwicklung der Sprachen - Linguistik contra Evolution, 2. Auflage, Holzgerlingen 2007 (Erstauflage: 2003).
- Vertaling van Hosea, in: G. de Koning: Hosea actueel, Gods liefde en trouw, Doorn 2003, p. 8-36.
- Vertaling van Joël, in: G. de Koning: Joël actueel, God bestuurt de geschiedenis, Doorn 2003, p. 8-19.
- Vertaling van Amos, in: G. de Koning: Amos actueel, Gods toorn over de zonde, Doorn 2006, p. 9-28.
- Sprachenreden oder Zungenreden? Bielefeld 2006 (online: clv.de).

About the Author

Dr Roger Liebi (Dipl. Mus., B.Th., M.Th., Th.D.), was born in 1958, and is married with six children, studied the languages of the Biblical world (Greek, classical, modern Hebraic, Aramaic, and Akkadian), as well as theology. He works as a speaker, Bible Teacher, and lecturer (Archaeology and the environment of Old Testament) in various countries. Due to his many years of expertise with the Scriptures and related fields, he has published a series of books (cf. his bibliography) Topics covered include: exegesis, culture studies, the origin of languages, prophecy, Israel, archaeology and Christian apologetics. He has participated in three projects as a Bible translator.

Are we really living in the last days?
More than 175 fulfilled prophecies

Roger Liebi
380 pages, hardcover, 2012
$ 19,00
ISBN: 978-3-943175-08-0

The Biblical term "End Times" does not involve the end of the world. Rather, what is meant by "End Times" is the end of the long period between the First and Second Coming of Jesus Christ.

According to the Bible the "End Times" will essentially be characterized by the Jews' return from the worldwide Diaspora to the Land of their Forefathers (1882 until the present) and by the new founding of the State of Israel (1948), after a long period of interruption.

In this book the author deals with more than 175 Biblical prophecies which all refer to the "End Times." These predictions have been demonstrably fulfilled in our era of world history: from 1882 until the present.

From this clear proof can be provided that we are actually living in the "End Times" and Jesus Christ will soon come as King and Judge of the world!

The Messiah in the Temple
The Symbolism and Signifiance of the
Second Temple in Light of the New Testament

Roger Liebi
656 pages, hardcover, 2012
$ 39,00
ISBN: 978-3-943175-05-9

This full colour volume, originally published in German, has now
been translated into English to reach
a wider audience. Its author, ROG-
ER LIEBI, is a Messianic Jew, and,
as such, is ideally placed to bring
out the symbolism and significance
of the Second Temple in the light
of the New Testament. The book is
beautifully illustrated, with many
photographs, diagrams, and artis-
tic impressions that guide the read-
er through the difference parts of the Temple as it would have
looked in the days the Lord walked in its precincts. As the
writer says in the introduction, "The intention of this book is
to lead the reader into the world of the Gospels and the Acts
of the Apostles, the epoch in which the Old and New Testaments meet and unite together in fulfilment of the divine
promise of salvation". If you want to get a deeper insight into
aspects of the life and ministry of the Lord and the apostles,
then this fascinating book will reward the patient and dili-
gent reader. Its thorough research and detailed indexing will
enable the student to access material that helps to bring the
word of God to life. Others may be drawn by the extensive
use of illustrations, which, with the accompanying text, will
give insights into favourite passages.

Through the Eyes of the Prophet
World History according to Daniel

Roger Liebi
126 pages, paperback, 2014
$ 9,00
ISBN: 978-3-943175-31-8

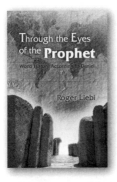

Is world history the sum of every coincidence? Are we at the mercy of blind Fate? Products of "random chance" in the infinite dimensions of the universe?

Many philosophical systems and ideologies put forward particular views of history. Yet all these systems of thought offer only speculation regarding the question of the future. Roger Liebi refers to the one Book which makes a fundamentally different claim. A Book with detailed prophecy which extends over millennia and yet is infallibly fulfilled. With the help of the prophet Daniel, Roger Liebi shows us a concrete view of the future whose reliability and precision are supported impressively by over 200 fulfilled prophecies on the subject of world history.

Christlicher Medienvertrieb
Hagedorn
Postfach 30 04 30
D-40404 Düsseldorf
Germany
www.cmv-duesseldorf.de
info@cmv-video.de